Civil War Letters and Diary of Andrew H. Gale of the 137th Regiment New York State Volunteers

Collected and compiled by Richard T. Gillespie

*Continued good reading in
your interest in the Civil War*

Richard T. Gillespie

HERITAGE BOOKS
2005

HERITAGE BOOKS

AN IMPRINT OF HERITAGE BOOKS, INC.

Books, CDs, and more—Worldwide

For our listing of thousands of titles see our website
at
www.HeritageBooks.com

Published 2005 by
HERITAGE BOOKS, INC.
Publishing Division
65 East Main Street
Westminster, Maryland 21157-5026

International Standard Book Number: **0-7884-3278-8**

Dedicated to Mrs. Mildred "Mid" Overpeck, great-niece of Andrew H. Gale, for the loan of the letters and diaries from which this book was compiled; also to my very patient wife, Joan, who spent many lonely hours during this project.

Table of Contents

Introduction vii

Chapter One   Clouds of War 1

Chapter Two   Mustering In 19

Chapter Three   Andrew H. Gale returns home 29

Chapter Four   Continuation of life at home 51

Chapter Five   Andrew's Return to War 65

Chapter Six   September 1863 Move to The West 91

Chapter Seven   November and December-1863 115

Chapter Eight   To the War's End: 1865 143

Index 173

Introduction

Nearly one hundred and forty years have passed since the last shot was fired in the great struggle between the North and the South, sometimes referred to as, "The War of the Rebellion": the American Civil War. But even today, stories describing the battles and the men who fought them still surface, as they will for years to come. Interest in the Civil War has never waned. In fact, it seems to grow as the years pass by. Motion pictures such as "The Civil War," "North and South," "Gettysburg," and "Andersonville," have been produced and are frequently rerun on national television, and new books such as this one are constantly being published. Historians continue to search for artifacts throughout the areas where battles took place. At the present time there is a major project underway off the coast of North Carolina to recover the ironclad U.S.S. *Monitor* from the Atlantic Ocean. The turret has been raised from the bottom of the ocean and is being restored in The Mariner's Museum in Newport News, Virginia. On the last day of the year 1863, while under tow off Hatteras Island during a storm, the *Monitor* sank, taking four officers and twelve of the crew with her. Thus far, along with the turret, the anchor has been retrieved and underwater archaeologists from the National Oceanic and Atmospheric Administration, together with the Mariner's Museum, are now attempting to raise her gun. Another salvage operation is about to begin in the Pasquatank River at Elizabeth City, North Carolina, to recover a Confederate gunship that had been part of a six-ship fleet of small ships that tried to defend Elizabeth City from Union forces. All six ships were either sunk or scuttled during the battle. This ship was found lying not too far under the surface of the river, buried in the sand.

The fascination that many hold for the Civil War will be a long time in dying, and as old trunks are uncovered in attics across the United States, new versions of old stories will be told by descendants of those who fought the battles, as well as scholars and historians of similar interests.

For many years after the close of hostilities between the states, souvenirs and artifacts were found over all of the areas where fighting took place. Farmers, researchers, sightseers, picnickers, and just plain folks from everywhere in the country dug up relics and mementos carried into the war by soldiers from both sides. Guns, muskets, swords, bullets, canteens, caps and parts of uniforms, bayonets and many more such items were found on battlefields such as Antietam, Gettysburg, the Wilderness, Fredericksburg and others. A farmer plowing a field near Gettysburg would unearth part of a cap and ball pistol; a young scout troop would find a Confederate canteen in a field outside of Fredericksburg; a hiker on a weekend camping trip would find a spent bullet lodged in the trunk of an old oak tree in Georgia; and Civil War buffs would spend weekends scouring the many battlefields for souvenirs of the great American Civil War.

As the years pass, fewer and fewer of these treasures are found. Today a rare discovery of one kind or another is still made but they happen rather infrequently. Now the Civil War memories are coming from a different source, a source that has not yet dried up, as have the hardware items of the past. The mobility of our present society has caused many of us to lighten our possessions from one move to the next and in doing so, we are finding that we just can't carry Great Uncle Harry's old trunk with us any longer. We thus decide to go through it one last time to see what we will keep, what we will sell at the flea market, or what we will just throw away. It is from these trunks and attics that we occasionally find a prized box of letters or a diary written by a Civil War soldier to his family and loved ones at home, along with letters that he received while in the army. It was customary for many a fighting man of the day to retain the letters from home and then send them home at the end of the year, along with the diary he kept. From the trunks and attics of relatives and kinfolk of those who were involved in the struggle come articles such as letters, clothing, diaries, newspapers, and firsthand accounts of marches and battles. Handwritten stories of the battles, the days leading up to the conflicts, the aftermath, the time off and everything about the Civil War are there for the historians and the enthusiasts to read.

I have recently made a discovery of this type while assisting some friends prepare to move into a retirement village. A trunk that had followed them around for over fifty years of married life contained the items mentioned above. They had belonged to a great-uncle of the wife and other relatives of the husband. You cannot know the feeling that comes from sitting down with a diary dated 1863 or 1864 and seeing, in the handwriting style of that era, the exact words and thoughts of someone who was there in the thick of such historic events. In my case, this find included letters from six different Union soldiers from five different regiments. The word-for-word transcriptions of these letters and diaries, as well as the regimental, platoon and company records obtained from the National Archives, New York State Archives, New York State Library and other repositories, are what make up the chapters of this book. Reading the letters that were sent home to the families, describing army life and relating the perils and dangers of each battle to mother and dad or sister or wife, is like taking advantage of the use of a time machine. You can travel back in years and almost relive the events through the eyes of those who were there.

Having grown up in York, Pennsylvania, only twenty-five miles east of Gettysburg, I have always had an intense interest in the Civil War. As a young boy of eight, in July of 1938 I was privileged to attend with my family the 75th Anniversary of the Battle of Gettysburg. It was a weeklong celebration with military ceremonies and dedications of great magnitude. One of my fondest memories of this event was meeting with and talking to some of the many veterans of the war still living at that time. Veterans from both the North and the South attended. On hand were 1359 Union veterans along with 486 Confederate veterans. Those men were housed in a tent city set up on the battlefield, and the old soldiers passed their spare time seated in front of their tents, discussing, in a friendly manner, their experiences on those three fateful July days in 1863, seventy-five years earlier. As a boy of eight, I could not fathom at that time that I was actually participating in a part of history, but as the years have passed, the impact has grown. I possibly met with some of the men who are mentioned in the following chapters of this book.

As the years have gone by, my personal interest in the Civil War has grown. I have spent many hours touring the battlefields throughout the East and South. Many books have been written, of which I have read quite a few, but not all. These books told of the battles and the major leaders of the two opposing forces and were, and still are, very informative to those of us who want to learn more about this phase of our American history. In my travels and studies I spent much time looking for items of interest to give me closer personal ties to the actual events of those war years of 1861-65. Among the trophies I have been able to obtain are a Union officer's sword and a Confederate "Richmond" rifle, which hangs over the fireplace in our family room.

The letters and diaries used to compile this book were acquired from the great-niece of Andrew H. Gale, a young Union soldier from Groton, New York. He was a member of Company K of the 137th Regiment, N.Y.S.V. (New York State Volunteers). It is Company K that will be heard from most in the following pages, since the majority of the letters and diaries are from members of that unit. Through letters and diaries written by Andrew H. Gale and his uncle, Ezra Bostwick, also of Company K, the movements and activities, including battles and Army transfers, will be traced for the entire duration of the war, from 1862 until late 1865.

The letters from members of the 137th Regiment relate tales of battles as well as the conditions the Civil War soldier had to endure to carry out his orders and duties. Although the reports are all from the Union side of the conflict, there have been many similar narrations from the Confederate position, and in the latter stages of the hostilities, the Southern soldier suffered even great difficulties, due to being overwhelmed by large numbers of better equipped adversaries.

Over the winter of 1861 and spring of 1862, the Union leaders made plans to move on Richmond, the capitol of the Confederacy, and to destroy General Joseph Johnston's Southern Army. The Northern troops were stronger, better equipped, and more numerous than those of the South and the Union commander was given orders to begin an offensive. This was to become known as the Peninsular Campaign.

The Federal Army had been under the command of Major General Irvin McDowell since the beginning of the war, until the Union defeat at Bull Run. Then President Lincoln summoned Major General George B. McClellan to the Capitol and promoted him to commander of all Union forces in the Washington area. McClellan took command on

July 26, 1861, under Commander-in-Chief of the Union Armies, Lieutenant General Winfield Scott.

McClellan was a West Point graduate who had served in the Mexican War, but he had resigned from the Army in 1857 to become a railroad executive. Even now he was only thirty-four years old but was well respected as a superior organizer.

McClellan believed that by creating a large, well-trained army, he could lead them into Virginia and capture Richmond, the new capitol of the Confederacy, and end the war almost before it got started.

Although President Abraham Lincoln had given him a direct order on January 26, 1862, to begin his offensive on Richmond, McClellan kept requesting more troops and supplies and did not begin to make his move until early March. This lapse in time gave the Southern commanders the time they needed to build up their forces, and took away much of the numerical superiority held earlier by the Union Army.

Maj. Gen. George B. McClellan

Chapter One

As the clouds of war approached over the horizon, many men on both sides of the struggle, began their preparations for what they knew was coming. States in both the North and South put out the call for volunteers, to mobilize for the pending conflict. These units grew slowly until the morning of April 12, 1861, the day the South fired on the Union forces manning Fort Sumpter, in Charleston Harbor, South Carolina. What had been the Federal Army, before the outbreak of hostilities, was made up of men from all of the states, including those in the South. As fighting began, those men from the states seceding from the Union, returned to their homes in the south to join Regiments being formed by the Confederacy. Both armies began small and had to build. The North had to replace those officers and men lost to the South, and the Southern states were building an army from scratch. On April 15th, President Lincoln issued a call for 75,000 volunteers to serve for three months. Fighting units were formed in many ways, but one of the most successful ways was for local and state regiments to be enlisted from various cities and towns through out the north. Since the majority of people in the North assumed the war would last only a short time, three month enlistments were all that were required. Usually some wealthy businessman or a retired military officer, would request permission, from the Federal Government, to organize a regiment for federal service. One such regiment was the 137th Regiment of Infantry from central New York State. On August 31, 1862, Colonel David Ireland asked for, and was granted, authority to recruit this regiment. He began his drive for volunteers in Binghamton and it was from there that they were mustered into Federal service on September 25th and 26th, 1862, for a three year tour of duty. The companies that comprised the regiment were recruited from towns such as Binghamton, Sanford, Conklin, Kirkwood, Richford, Union, Windson, Owego, Ithica, Chenabgo, Lisle, Maine, Triangle, Groton, Spencer, Candor, Barton, and Elmira. Company K was made up of men from Groton, Danby and Caroline. The 137th Regiment, N.Y.S.V., left Binghamton, N.Y., on September 27, 1862, to begin its service, which would last until the men were mustered out of service, as a unit, on June 9, 1865, near Bladensburg, Md.

The regiment was marched, immediately, to Harpers Ferry, Virginia, remained there until September 30th, and then moved to Bolivar Heights, Virginia, where it spent the months of October and November in training. Bolivar Heights became its base during most of December. The Regiment took part in a few actions from there. Andrew H. Gale, a twenty one year old member of the 137th Regiment, was a farmer from near Groton, New York, who like many other young men of his age, and younger, enlisted in the army when the regiment recruiters came to Groton. He enlisted in Company K, on August 15. He volunteered for three years service and left New York state on the above mentioned date, when the entire regiment shipped out.

Not long after arriving in Virginia, Andrew received his first letter from the folks at home, who included his Father, Peter Gale, his mother, Chloe Gale, his sister, Agusta Gale and his younger brother, Scott, a baby.

Union Army Training Camp

Thursday, Sept 25, 1862

My dear boy Andrew. I got home safe. We called to Wms and took breakfast or dinner and found all the folks well. I suppose Aaron Pick will come out tomorrow and I thought I would write a few lines to you. I should like to see you first rate tonight and see you well. Send a line by Pick and let us know how you get along, Your Mother is afraid you are sick. Take good care of yourself. I will send a little book to you. Paruse it carefully, particularly the cover. Cora gave it to me for you. Your Mother will send you a shirt. Amelia and Frank has been here, they came the day or night we went away. They have gone to Etna. Frank is the same old sixpence. Amelia is not so jovel. She was here the night you was to the ball. I hope you will not attend any more while you are to the war. I don't want to deprive you of innocent enjoyment but it seems a solumn time to me when our country is bleeding amd so many of our noble boys are suffering and dying of sickness and wounds, the casulties of the battlefield. I feel more like weeping but it is best to be cheerful but not in vain--Mary and Helen have been over here since we got home. If you are sick and not able to go with them come home and I will meet you to Courtland and take good care of you till you get well but I hope you are not going to be sick. You must take good care of your uncle Stephen and keep him out of the guard house. Our love to you and all the best to the boys.

A. H. Gale   P. B. Gale
(father)

The letter that follows is Andrew's first letter home, since leaving his family and friends in Groton

Sunday evening Oct 5th/62

Dear Parents   I thought
I would write a few lines to you. I have been busy today
although it is the first Sunday that has seemed like the Sabbath.
We have moved our tents today. We come from Frederic City
night before last. We got here after dark, we slept on the side
hill that night. The next day we had marching orders at two
oclock. We moved about a mile to camp. We are now
stationed near Sundy Hook, Va.[1] We have just been on dress
parade. The days are rather short. There is signal flag on a
mountain west of us. They have a place that on the flag is
black with a white spot in it. In the night they have a
light. They have certain movement. They have been swinging
the flag most all day.That is the way they telegraph in this
country. They have several flag stations along the mountain.
The one west of us they say that they can see Stonewall
Jackson's army. They can telegraph in that way from McClellan
Army to Washington. I was on guard last night. There is a
large army around here. They were the fourth reserves of
McClellan under Banks.[2]The boys have got supper   ready so I
must bring my letter to a close We live very well. We have
army crackers, coffee, bacon, rice, sugar, black tea, molasses
and beans. I am very well satisfied out here. When you write
send the number of the Regiment that Mead is in and where he
is & where the boys are of the Auburn regiment that was taken
prisoners. Write soon.

---

[1]Sandy Hook. Va

[2]Maj. Gen. Nathanial P. Banks, former Republican Speaker of the House of
Representatives, who used his influence to obtain his commission

From your son Andrew
Directions Co. K   137th Reg, N.Y.S.V.
Care Col. David Ireland
Washington, D.C.

Further correspondence between Andrew Gale and his family continue.

Groton, Oct. 12th 1862

Dear Andrew   I received your letter last
Saturday and one a week ago Saturday and was very glad to
hear from you and the boys and I want to hear from you at
least every week. I should written to you last week but
the girls were here when I got your letter and they said they
would write to you and so I excused myself on that ground,
pretty slim excuse. I will try to write often I want you to
whether I do or not. Your Mother is gone to meeting tonight.
Lois & Nathan came down and left their children here and
have gone to meeting. Nathan sends his respects to you.
Harvey, Hellen and Mary got letters from you last week.
Welber got one from L and one from John Ludlow last night.
John is at or near Chicago. He says they are closely guarded
but he says some of the boys sckedaddled most every night. I
heard he wrote to her folks that he should be home next week.
He has not forgotten his old trick. He wrote of being taken
prisoner and how scared some were. I wonder if J was
not some scared. Mead is in the Co. C Col-Dwight, 160
Regiment N.Y.S.V.Mead is at home now, is to go to Auburn in
the morning if he is well enough. He has been sick a few days.
He ate to many beans. He says they have marching orders next
Wednesday and are going to New York and from there to New
Orleans by water. His coat is like yours but his pants are light
blue like the first uniform. Their Col. Is that man that spoke to

Groton about a year ago, the time you rode up with Zack. Harvey is at home to work now days. His father could not get any help and he had to come home. Help is rather scarce just now. I have got our corn cut up. The north piece is first rate and the pumpkins can't be beat between here and Ithica. I counted between two rows of stauks, North and South over 125 pumpkins. Beat that if you can in Dixy. Directions of the Reg that John is in is Co. I, 111-Reg N.Y.S.V., Camp Douglas, Chicago, Ill. I got a letter from Egbert and his father last night. They are well. Frank is out here. James has got a winter job on reapers and he wont come out this fall. Williams Laverona is here but expects to go home tomorrow. She wants to know if her pa is not going to write to her. She is well and so are all our folks. Mr Wescott is some better. Your Grandmother has been there most of the time since he has been sick. Betsey L is most scared to death about her daddy as she calls him. Willy fetched your grandmother home this morning and now she is going to dry my apples. Write good long letters and all the news. You write the days are pretty short. I suppose the nights are rather long when you have to stand on guard or sleep on the ground. You did not write that you have not got your knapsack yet, but I conclude you have not for I have not seen any envelopes or stamps. Our folks have all gone to bed and I must close but if you was here I would build another fire and set up a spell longer for I don't feel sleepy when you write. Write about the boys for they all want to hear from them. Stephens wife and Ida was here today and we had or 4 letters from Dixie and had pretty good times. Uncle Joe came over to see your letter and if you get spare time send him a letter. It would please him. We heard by the daily yesterday that the rebels were in Penna after horses. My paper is full. Good night

    A. H. Gale   From   P. B. Gale

Oct. 20/62

Dear Sister,

I received your letter tonight just as I was going on dress parade. We are encamped near Knoxvill, Maryland. Maybe you can find it on the map. It is down the river from harpers ferry. We are in a valley. There is several regiments encamped near here. We don't have much to do. We have to drill two hours in the afternoon & at half past five we have a dress parade. We have meeting Sunday. Yesterday we had only prayer. When the preacher got through praying it commenced raining so we run to our tents then we went on dress parade. It commenced raining again then we run to our tents again. It was quite stormy last night. It was a fine day today. I should like to be home so you could see me & I could see you and the rest of the folks & crack butternuts with you. We have black walnuts & chestnuts here. We have to clear rebels farms here. We have got our street as clean as a dooryard. When we go into a lot to encamp we strike our tents. We put them about twenty five tents to the rows. The tents in the rows are about three feet apart. The company next to..put theirs in the same way with the back of their tents about three feet from ours. Then the streets are dug and scooped until the grass & weeds are all taken off then we have to sweep the streets every morning. We have straw to sleep on. It is rather cool here in the night. We sleep very comfortable but if we have to stay here through the winter we will have to have different arrangements. They say that we are a going to have round tents some like the Indians tents. Excuse all the mistakes & bad writing. Write soon

from Andrew

This is a letter from Peter Gale, Andrew's father, to Andrew. It is the first time that Andrew's Uncle Ezra, also a member of the 137th Regiment, N.Y.S.V., is mentioned.

Groton Oct. 26-1862

Dear Andrew

Hellen received a letter from you last week and we learned from that that you had not received anything from us since you left Binghamton. We have two letters and now we will try another. John Sharpstein got a letter from you and said he was going to answer it today. We are all anxious to hear from you often and if Uncle Sam will carry my letters you shall hear from us often for I can immagine how you feel to not hear from us when the mail comes in. We often think of you especially when it rains and I believed it has rained once in twenty four hours for the last two weeks. It has rained all day today steady without any recess and it freezes some so the trees are pretty well loaded. I hope it will be good weather by and by. Tell Ezra that I took the shoes off his colt and he is doing well. Silas Low sold his other horse together with one of his for $150, so John Sharpstein told me. It rains hard now. Scott and his mother has gone to bed and to sleep. Augusta sits by me looking on while I am writing. Grandmother has just gone to bed and sends her love to Ezra-you and L. She says they hasn't one of them wrote a word to her. Augusta sends her love to you and wants you to write something to her and Scott

wants Andrew to have his love and he wants to know if
Andrew has got a furlough to come home. He says he would
like to see you very much.

Oct. 29

When Scott got up this morning I told him what I had written
to you for him. He said why didn't you write the other I said
what, having forgotten some that he told me. He said you
know. I want to put my arms around his neck and kiss him. He
missed you as much as any of us. We read a paper and a song
or two from I suppose. This morning looked rather dismal. The
ground was covered with snow and it snowed quite smart most
all day a little and tonight it will freeze pretty hard. Today I
commenced chopping wood. The old wood pile is used up but
I don't have to draw it. Harris Bostwick was here tonight and
said they were all well.. He has been thrashing all the fall in
Genoa. He feels a little uneasy about the draft. They have some
25 to make out in Locke. Harris said Ludlow had heard that
John was sick.

    Tuesday   It is fine morning. The sun shining
through the icecles make a fine appearance but the snow is fast
melting away. We think some of going to Hirams today to get
some peaches. They sent for us to come. Augusta is twisting
yarn. We are all well.

    A.H. Gale   From your Parents   P. B. Gale

C. M. Gale

    Dear Son,   We seen Hellen letter and we was glad to
hear you was well. We wrote too letters to you and you have
not received any. Wilber rote to you that you friends was
making great advice because you was gone to the war. What
would you think of your father and mother and grandmother
and the rest of your friends if we did not feel bad and
loanesime. Don't worry about that fore we made up our mind
not to worry. Make yourself contented about that we wot

(want) to see you very much. We was glad to hear that you
would try to come home this winter.   Chloe M. Gale
                Andrew H. Gale

At the beginning of the war, there was no Draft and manpower
for the Union Army relied on those already serving in the army, and
recruits and those volunteering for army life. The Draft was to begin
on February 15, 1862 but was postponed from that date.

                        Groton, Nov. 9th, 1862
Dear Andrew
                as the rest has written I guess I will write a little. We
got your letter Saturday the 8th and was glad to hear from you.
Mr Davison and his wife was over here. We are glad to hear
from the boys. We are all well and have enough to do to keep
us out of mischief. I have not got my corn husked and I am not
the only one. Reuben Igafs is the only one that has got his fall
work done. Harvey come home to help him and is going to
school again. He talks of commencing tomorrow. He is going
to room and do chores to Stephen Bostwicks. He promised to
help me this week but I guess I shall have to do my own work.
We have had quite a cold snap, it froze pretty hard.The talk is
that the 100 Reg is going to leave Auburn, Wednesday and go
to Texas.Barier K said that Hellen King said she saw it in Barer
Kings Auburndaily, Saturday---and the talk is the 111th is
coming to Auburn. It is all excitement here about the draft.
Most of them has got a certificate. I reckon the plank board
has been doing pretty good business for the week part for most
everyone won't out to get their names taken off. Harris
Bostwick and all the nine/ theys all the Harris's. Samuel
Greenleaf and I heard tonight that it is all illegal in the way it
has been managed. I think it ought to be. Monday, Nov. 10
The draft is postponed till the fifteenth I believe. We have lost

our election and the bunnies feel so much elated over their late success but we must wait till our soldiers get home and then we will try them again. Locke and Groton went pretty large for Wadsworth but New York City is what told the story. It went over 3100 for Seymore. It must be a real grog hole. Tell Ezra I went to Genoa to see Hewet but he was gone to New York but his wife and her father was there. I paid in the money, had it endorsed on the mortgage and took a receipt. Ask Ezra if he has got that mortgage on record that he took off the Irishman.

Wednesday, the 12th.   Us folks and Mrs Davison and Grandmother had some things packed to send by P. Wright but I suppose you have heard before this time that Mr Wright has concluded not to go to Dixie, so we fetched the things home again. If you want some things sent, write what things you want and where you want them sent to. I will send you one dollar at a time. I will send again soon.Grandmother says to tell Ezra to be contended foe she will send him lots of things by and by. Slocums barn burned last night. We saw the light this morning. He lived on the corner below Hirams. It took fire from a pipe.
Goodby From Your Father with love   P. B. Gale

The Military Draft did not begin on November 15th, as stated in Peter Gale's letter above, but was again postponed.

Groton, Nov. 17th/62
Dear Andrew.   We received your letter Saturday. Every letter we have received from you came in Saturday. Your Mother and I was down to Groton Saturday to carry a few things to put in a box Mrs Fisher was going to send to her husband and if you get the things you will probably hear from us again. Nathan has written to Ezra what things we sent and if you get them write what things you received and if you need

anything more for your comfort that we can send to you. Write to us what it may be. If you need a comforter to sleep under to keep you warm and if you can carry it from place to place, we will send you one. We will divide with a soldier but we might be a little partial who it was but I think I could harber and feed any of them and we should be perfectly delighted to feed some of them around our table you better believe but we cannot have the privilege. We will try to send some little comforter once is a while if you have the luck to get them. I got two letters from Mr Davison from L Sat. Davison's folks are well. When I was to meeting last night I thought of some familiar faces that was not there but I hope you have religious teaching and I hope you will prophet by it and learn piety and be a christian while you may for you know not what a day may bring forth. The draft is postponed indefinately and it may not take effect at all but it has affected some verry sensibly. Some it has given a thirst for education. Jack went to Auburn to get his name off the roll but did not succeed and they say he enlisted under Prof Bauldwin---Senior got clear by going out twice. James Wallace has schedadled to parts unknown. He and Anne Main I heard, had gone off together. You wrote that you wish you were here to help me husk my corn. I wish you was for help is scarce. It has rained most all day and is as dark as a contraband. Nelson B. and Mary G--Silas L and Laura Milegar has been on a visit to Auburn. Almina has got home. James & folks are well and so are all our folks.   P. B. Gale

     Tuesday morning. It has stoped raining and is foggy and warm and we are about ready for breakfast and all appears to be well. We wish you could be here to eat with us. I sent a letter to you last week with a dollar in it and I will send a dollar in this and your grandmother will send a dollar for Ezra and we all send our love and good wishes to you and our friends in the army. From your   affectionate father
     A. H. Gale   P. B. Gale

Andrew Gale was receiving the latest news, of home, from his parents and sister, but due to his moving around from one camp to another, and for various other reasons, it took him until late November to get a letter off to the folks at home.

Boliver Hights, Sunday-Nov. 22/62

Dear Parents   I received your letter last night & was glad to hear from you. Some of your letters come in Saturday, but as a general thing, they come through in three or four days. I am glad to hear that some victuals are on the road for me. I think they will come good. We have not received it yet. I guess it will come in tomorrow or next day if you sent it on the express. If you sent me a box that is if you direct it to me, send it by express & take a reciept & send it to me & if the box gets miscarried or lost, I can get pay for it. We live more decent than we have since we left Binghamton. If a man was he had to bound himself or go without eating anything. We have bread to eat now instead of hardtack. We draw potatoes & dried apples. I have apple sauce a good share of the time. There is but four in our tent now. When we were in pleasant Valley, we had six, one has gone to Frederic to the General Hospital, that is Gilsmoe & uncle Ezra is in the hospital here. He is very sick. I wrote to Davisons folks that was there but L has come out & Ezra gone in his place. He received two letters last night. One was from uncle Nathan. I am very well satisfied with what you sent me. You know I like honey. I tell you when you send anything more. I expect you will if I live. I want you to send me some tea & paragoric. I have quite the belly ache tonight. There is not much going on here it is the old story. All quiet of the Potomac. I was on picket last week campground to. I had some milk, some of the boys went after a hog but they could not find any. The hogs on the picket line has to suffer & some of the cows get milked. I reckon there has been three of this

13

regiment taken prisoner. They were out after spies over the lines. Some of the 149th boys got taken prisoner. They were out after a hog. The Rebs don't like to have our pickets forage beyond the lines. If they do they nab them if they get a good chance. I wrote to you that Mike Amadon had made us a call. If uncle Nathan mentioned it in his letter telling what regiment he was in. He is but a little ways from us. They are in the same Brigade with us. If they (uncle Nathans folks) want to write a letter to him they can send it to me with two envelopes & I will take it to him. I should like to hear from them myself. Tell all friends to write for I can't think of all as there is not much news. I will have to close. I have wrote three besides this today & evening.Please write soon, excuse all the mistakes & bad writing for my writing desk is my knapsack. From your affectionate son   Andrew.
Please excuse for not filling out the sheet.

                            Dear Sister.   I received your letter over a week ago & was glad to hear from you. I am sitting in my tent tonight by a good fire nearly as warm as the one you are sitting by. We have a fireplace in our tent that keeps it warm most of the time. We draw new tents tomorrow they say. There is not much to write about now. I should like to be at home & take dinner with you but thats not to be very soon. We live very well here but I expect to feast some when that box comes. You may bet that things from home will relish well. Give my love to all, to mother, father, & Scott. guess you may give my love to Augusta & all inquiring friends. I must bring my letter to a close for I feel tired. I have wrote most all day.   From your affectionate Brother.
                          Andrew to Augusta
            please write soon & oblige.

                    Groton, Nov 22nd, 62

Dear Andrew;   As your mother has written her letter and they have all gone to bed, I take this opportunity to write a few lines to you. It is a source of great pleasure to me to peruse letters from you and undoubtly it is to you to hear from home. You wrote to Hellen that you did not hear from home often. This, I think is the fourth letter I have written but it may be you have not gotten them all. I do not mean to be slack about writing for I know it must be gratifying to hear from home and friends. Mr. Wright intends to leave Groton this week for the seat of war and I and folks intend to send some things to you. He is very kind in offering to take them. It is a pleasure to us to get a chance to send even some small articles to you. I should like to send you some apples. We have an abundance of them. The middle bins are full as high as your chin and half of the west bin and a lot in bags yet and some as nice as you ever saw. It may be we can send some but they are risky things to send in cold weather. I presume you have heard Gov. Delano is maried[3] and Adalene Bothwell is got to be Mrs. Harris. She was maried Friday night and we have had good weather ever since so I had a chance at least to get in my buckwheat and thrash it. It has been the worst fall for business I think I ever saw and the wind blows now for another storm. The 160th Reg has not left Auburn yet I believe. I saw Oliver Ashton last week. He said that Mead was well. Norman King and Dean Ammanion have got home. I heard the 111th Reg had been exchanged and had been sent back to Washington. Andrew Heath is gaining he says he wishes he was well and was exchanged for he cannot bear to have the boys go back without him. He says he likes soldering first rate. He is bent on seeing it out he says. John Ludlow will make a

---

"Married"

15

first rate soldier he says. John was not frightened as far as he could see at Harpers Ferry. They have got a first rate Captain but the Col., Andrew says he never wants to see his face again. We are just on the eve of an important election. One that we look to with as much interest if not more than any election since my day. The case is a fearful one on account of so many of the right stamp have gone to war. If the soldiers could vote it would be a clear case but if nothing happens I mean to do my part and wait the result. Mrs. Boswick and Ida was up here night before last. She had heard from Stephen most every day last week. She told us when Wright was going back and is going to send some things to Stephen if it does not get confiscated or stolen before it gets there. It is past ten and I must close for tonight. You must be a good boy, practice good morals. All well.

          From your father P. B. Gale   Andrew H.

          Monday morning.[4]   I thought I would write a little more. Those crackers, you have that are so hard they say you can soften them in cold water but I think I should like have them dry as cold and wet---when you write, write pretty heavy and don't fold your letter on a line for sometimes it becomes obliterated so it is difficult to read it, it being a pencil mark. Write often and a full letter if you have time. We are all well and hope you are enjoying the same blessing. Good by be a good boy, do as you would like to be done by and you will have friends. Although you are far from home be careful of your health as well as your morals. You are exposed to many temptations of which you must be ware. Cultivate good habits.

---

[4]Peter Gale continued the letter the next day

I hear so much about profane language and drinking in the army that it makes me tremble for the welfare of our friends. Our love to you and the boys.   P. B. Gale

Andrew Gale's parents were very concerned about his safety and continued to offer advice in all of their letters. This next letter, written by Andrew's mother, Chloe, was included with the above letter. It is the most touching of all of the letters in the book.

My Dear Son,   I would like to see you and talk with you about everything. I wish you was here to eat with us and stay with us. I don't want to complain. You have gone for a good cause. Be a good boy and try to be a good soldier. Allow me to say afew things to you that you may read when far away. The thought and feeling of your affectionate mother. It pains me to give you up but I do and your patriotism, the conviction of the country all told you must go to the war. Now you have gone to a strange land. Let me entreat you to look to a precious loving Savior who can help you in time of need. Let me exhort you to read the testiment which was given to you. Do not be ashamed to let your comrads know that you believe and reverence the scriptures to find some time each day to read a little of the word of God. It is the best companion you can find in all your loneliness and sorrows. You can find here a comforter and a friend. He speaks to you. Will you hear his voice and believe his word. Faith in God and a firm trust in him is better than all the bulwarks were built to shield the soldier from harm. I want you to be careful of your health. Give my love to Ezra and Stephen. From your affectionate mother

Chloe M. Gale   Andrew Gale

time since he has been sick Betsy
is most scared to death about her daddy
as she calls him Welly fetched your
grandmother home this morning and
now she is going to drying apples
write good long letters and all the news
you write the days are pretty short
I suppose the nights are rather long when
you have to stand on guard or lie
on the ground you did not write that
you have not got your knapsacks yet
but I conclude you have not for I had
not seen any envelopes that you took
from home yet if you want I should
send you any thing write and let
me know paper envelopes or stamps
our folks are all gone to bed and
I must close but if you was here
I would build another fire and
set up a spell longer I don't feel
sleepy when you write write about the
boys for they all want to hear from them
Stephens wife and Ida was here to day and
we had 3 or 4 letters from them and had
a pretty good time since you came out to
see your letter and if you got that
trunk send him a letter it would please
M deped by the sabby yesterday that the body
was in Penn after horses &c
my paper is full good night
AH Gale from — PB Gale

yours Oct 12th 1862
Dear Andrew I received your letter
last saturday and one a week ago saturday
day and was very glad to hear from
you and the boys and I want to
hear from you at least every week
I should written to you last week
but the girls were here when I got
your letter and they said they would
write to you and so I excused my
self on that ground pretty slim ex-
use I will try and write often
I want you to whether I do or not
your Mother is gone to meeting to
night Lois & Nathan came down
and left their children here and
have gone to meeting Nathan
sends his respects to you
Harvey Hellen and Mary got letters
from you last week Hellen got
one from L and one from John
Ludlow last night John is at a

Andrew Gale Letter Oct 12/62

Chapter Two

There are no further letters in December of 1862, from either Andrew or his family, and the next recorded personal contact does not happen until the middle of February, 1863. At that point, Andrew began keeping a daily diary of his activities. In the meantime, Regimental and Company K records trace the movements of the 137th Regiment, N.Y.S.V. The Company K Muster Roll card for Nov. & Dec., 1862, show that Andrew Gale was absent and a notation on the card, under remarks, stated, "Left sick at Harpers Ferry, Va. Dec. 10, '62". This same notation is carried on the Muster Roll for January & Feby, 1863.[5]

On a special Muster Roll taken April 10, 1863, Gale was still marked absent and under remarks it says, "*Sent to Hospital at Baltimore Dec. 10, 1862*".[5]

Muster cards for March & April, 1863, and May & June, 1863 both show him absent due to sickness since Harpers Ferry. As stated before, no personal contact, via letters or other correspondence, is made with Gale until February, when entries in his diary show him being at home on the farm in Groton, New York. It was the policy during this period, for soldiers to return home to recuperate from wounds and illness.

While Andrew H. Gale was at home in New York, Company K and the 137th Regiment, N.Y.S.V. continued fighting, as the following reports indicate. These records cover their travels and activities through the end of June, 1863 and leads right up to the battle at Gettysburg in early July.

Nov. 9, 1862 Near Rippon, Va.

National Archives Micro Film records

National Archives Micro Film records

Dec. 2, 1862 Charlestown, W Va
Dec. 6, 1862 Winchester, Va.
Dec. 9-16, 1862 Fairfax Station, Va
Dec. 27, 1862 Dumfees, Va.[7]

On December 1, they took part in an expedition to Winchester, Va., under the command of General John White Geary.[8] A note on the records stated, "which place we occupied"[9]

Maj. Gen. John W. Geary

---

[7]"A Compendium Of The War Of The Rebellion" by Frederick H. Dyer

[8]Brig. Gen. John White Geary, under command of General Hooker. "The Blue & The Grey"

[9]National Archives Micro Film records

Dec. 10. Rest of Company marched to Dumfries, Va., via Hillsboro, Strasburg, Green Spa, Fairfax. Counter marched from Dumfries at present camp Dec. 20

Dec. 27. Made march to reinforce Col. Corby at Dumfries. Encountered Stuarts Cavalry[10] a short distance beyond the Ocauquion River. Considerable skirmishing but no loss in Regt. Returned to camp Dec. 30.[11]

Jan. 1863. Return dated Aquine Creek. Feb. 1, 1863

Feb. 1863. Return dated Aquine Creek, Va. Mar. 2, 1863
Mar. 1863. Return dated Aquine Creek, Va.
Apr. 1863. Return dated Aquine Creek, Va.
May 1863 Return dated Aqua Creek Landing, Va.
June 1863. Not stated [12]

A third set of records is the 137th Regiment, N.Y.S.V. FIELD & STAFF Muster Roll.

Sept. 22-Oct. 31, 1862-Boliver Hts, Va. (signed) Oct. 31, 62. Lewis

Nov.-Dec. 1862 Changed station from pleasant Valley, Va to Bolivar Hts, Va

Oct. 1. Made march from camp the Charlestown on reconnaissance.

Dec. 1. Marched to and occupied Winchester, Va. via Berryville. Broke camp at Bolivar and marched to Dumfrees,

---

[0]General J.E.B. Stuart, Confederate Cavalry Commander

[1]137th Reg. N.Y.S.V. Regimental Clerk's Records

[2]137th Reg. N.Y.S.V. Regimental Clerk's Records

Va. via Hillsboro, Leesburg, Fairfax C. H.

Dec. 10. Countermarched to present camp. Arrived Dec. 20th.

Dec. 27 marched towards Dumfrees, Va. Encountered Stuarts Cavalry a short distance from the Occoquan River. Returned to camp Dec. 30.[13]

Sept. 25 to Oct 31, 1862..Bolivar Heights, Va...No entry

Nov. & Dec., 1862..Camp in the Pines near Fairfax Station, Va.. Nov. 9, 62. Made a successful reconnaissance to several miles beyond Charlestown and returned to our camp in Boliver Heights, Va. the same evening having marched 28 miles.

Dec. 2.. Started on an expedition to Winchester. Met the enemy's cavalry at Charlestown and Berryville but after a slight brush they retreated. We marched on to Winchester, formed in lines of battle, but finding no opposition, we entered the city, occupied the place about two hours then returned to Boliver Heights, Va via Bunker Hill midway Charlestown having marched 70 miles in five days.

Dec 10..Started from Boliver Heights. Passed through Leesburg, Fairfax C.H., and several other places. Arrived at Dumphreys on the 17th. (This is the third different spelling of

---

[13]National Archives micro film records-137th Reg. N.Y.S.V. Field & Staff Monthly Report

the town of Dunfrees, Va.) The next morning we were ordered back. Accordingly countermarched to this place.

Dec 27.. Started from our present camp at 10 o'clock P.M. And halted near the Occoquan River at 3 o'clock A.M. We met the enemy and drove them from the field. Passed on to within three miles of Dumphreys. Sent reinforcements to that place and on the 30th returned to our camp near Fairfax Station, Va.

As the year 1862 ended, the 137th Regiment, N.Y.S.V. was training and preparing for further battles, but Private Andrew H. Gale was not with them. The illness he had contracted at Harpers Ferry, in early December, was serious enough to send him home to Groton, New York, where he stayed until late June of 1863.

The year 1863 began as 1862 had ended. The 137th Regiment, N.Y.S.V. spent time training and preparing.

Jan.-Feb. 1863 Aquia Creek, Va, (signed) Feb. 28, 1863 While at Fairfax Station, Va. the Reg't was drilled in the Brigade and also Battalion drill each day. We started from camp Fairfax Station, Va. on Reconnaissance to Dumfrees, encountered the enemy (Stuart's Cavalry) at Dumfrees Plains, drove them in the loss and returned to camp on the 30th. Broke camp Fairfax Station. Jan 18. Marched via Dumfrees, Stafford C.H., Va to Aquia Creek. Since we have been here the men have been detached for fatigue duty and there has been no drilling.

April 10, 1863 Aquia Creek, Va. (Signed) April 10, 1863, Lewis

March & April 1863 Chancellorsville, Va April 30

May & June 1863 Littlestown, Pa. (signed) June 30, 1863

April 27, 1863. We broke camp at Aquia Creek, Va. and marched via Stafford C.H. To the Rappahannock River, crossed at Kelly's Ford and marched towards Fredericksburg, crossed the Rapidan & bivouacked for the night. Commenced marching about 8 A.M. The next morning in the direction of Fredericksburg. Found the enemy after about two hours march. Formed a line of battle and filed into the woods where we remained until about noon the next day. We advanced upon the enemy and drew them out in front of our batteries where they received murderous fire. We returned to our former positions and threw up Breastworks with but few tools that Bayonets and plates. A heavy fire of artillary commenced upon the morning of May 2 killing and wounding several of our men. The battle continued until May 4th. May 6th, 1863, we started for Aquia Creek, crossed the Rapahannock at the United States Ford, and marched, via Stafford C.H. Reaching Aquia Creek the 7th, where we remained, drilling each day that we were not engaged upon the Fortifications. We broke camp again at Aquia and marched to Stonemans Switch, to do guard duty, but soon after arriving there, received orders to march. We marched via Stafford C.H., Dumfrees, to Leesburg where we were detached from the Brigade to guard the bridge at Edwards Ferry. June 26, started again upon the march.[14] Crossed the Potomac & Monocacy Rivers, passed Point of Rocks and Petersville & encamped near Knoxville. June 28, started for Frederick City & reached there about sundown & bivouacked. June 29, marched through Walkerville,

---

[14]Dumfrees, Leesburg, Stafford C. H.. All located in Virginia

Woodbourough & Briceville. June 30 marched through Taneytown[15] to Littlestown[16] and encamped.[17]

Feb, 1863..near Aquia Creek, Va. This company has had but ten days drilling since the first day of January. Started from camp near Fairfax Station, Va., Jan 19/63 via Dumfries & Stafford Court House to this place arriving here Jan. 25/63. Since that time have been on Fatique Duty on the Dock and Fortifications with all available men we can muster. At present we are furnishing every well man for fortifications, guard & camp duty.

April 10, 1863..Aquia Creek, Va.   No entry

March & April, 1863..near Chancellorsville, Va. This company, with the Reg't have been stationed near Aquia Landing, Va. doing fatigue, guard and picket duty for the last two months.

May & June, 1863..Edwards Ferry, Va. This company, with the rest of the Regiment, started with the Army of the Potomac, on the 27th of April, crossed the Rappahannock & Rhapidan and arrived in Chancellorsville on the 30th. On the next morning advanced about three miles, found the enemy in force, fell back to our old position and through up breast

---

[5] Knoxville, Point of Rocks, Petersville, Frederick City, Walkerville, Woodborough, Briceville, and Taneytown are all located in Maryland.

[6] Littlestown, Pennsylvania

[7] National Archives micro film records-137th Regt. N.Y.S.V. Regimental records.

Union Quartermaster Workers at Aquia Crossing

works. The Brigade, being short of entrenching tools, Bayonets and plates were used instead of picks & shovels. On the 2nd of May we were not under fire, on the 3rd the Brigade was under an enfalading fire of grape and shell. Fortunately, none were wounded although our Regiment lost heavily. Received orders to retire, fell back in good order, took position near the Hospital. Four men, who were on picket in the evening of 2nd, were taken prisoners. On Monday of the 6th, recrossed the river and again Went into camp at Aquia Landing.[18]

These reports and pieces of correspondence, cover the time from the Mustering in of the 137th Regiment, N.Y.S.V., in August of

---

[18]National Archives micro film records-Co. K, Muster Roll records

1862, up to the end of June 1863. All of the military records, to this date, show that the regiment went from civilian life directly to the battlefield in a very short period of time. What training and drilling they got was given to them between battles and actions.

The main subject of this narrative, Pvt. Andrew H. Gale, a member of Compant K, of the 137th Regiment, N.Y.S.V., was involved in the movements and skirmishes from October until early December, 1862. At that time, according to Regimental and Company K records, he was sent to the Hospital in Baltimore due to illness.

There were no further letters, either, at that point in time and Andrew Gale did not begin keeping a diary until February, 1863. He began this from home in Groton, to where he returned from the hospital.

Chapter Three

As the 137th Regiment traversed the southern country side, following the Confererate Armys, from skirmish to skirmish, Andrew Gale, due to illness, of unknown origin, was sent from Harpers Ferry, Va. to a hospital in Baltimore, Md. From the records and information, obtained in the family and military data, it is not know just when he left the hospital and why he returned to Groton, New York. In some of his letters written to Andrew, Peter Gale, Andrew's father, had stated wishes to the effect that he had wished Andrew could come home and help with work around the farm. Andrew might have decided to do just that. The first word that was found was in his 1863 diary and it was recorded on February 3rd. Up until that point in time, the pages of the diary are completely blank.

Andrew's life at home was a perfectly normal one. His daily activities seem to be the same as any other civilian of the day, completing the chores around the farm. He gives no indication that a war is going on in another part of the country, nor that he had been a part of it only a few months ago.

He does what needs to be done, assisting his father on the farm. He visits relatives that live nearby and pals around with old buddies who are still in Groton. He even dates the local girls and attends church meeting on Sundays, with his family.

To recall, Andrew's immediate family consisted of his father Peter, mother Chloe, Sister Augusta, and baby brother Scott. The Gale family lived with Mrs Gale's mother, Ruth Bostwick, Andrew's Grandmother and their major occupation was farming.[19] Young Gale tended to numerous chores daily, before he could participate in any other activities. His being twenty one years old did not excuse him from assisting with the work to be done.

---

[9]1860 Federal Census. Town of Groton, N.Y., County of Tompkins

According to the entries in the diary for the next few months, it can be seen that much of the spare time was spent visiting with relatives living in the area. Almost every day, Andrew would make a short trip to see an uncle, an aunt or a friend. He had one special friend, "Harve", who was also home from the army, with whom he spent many hours touring the countryside.

Here is a closer look at Andrew H. Gale's entries in his diary during the year 1863.

Tuesday, February 3, 1863

pleasant. Gilispie John helped father saw some wood in the afternoon. Father went to the hollow. Took mother & Grandmother to uncle Stephens to stay the   evening. Helen come over here and stayed all night. It commenced snowing & blowing just at night & our folks came home almost froze

Wednesday, February 4, 1863

Pleasant this morning. Got up very late it being very cold now. Sheldon stoped in on his way to school to get warm he being very cold. Received a letter from Frank Smith. Father thrashed some today with the horses. I went over to the shed & fed the sheep so called to uncle Brians & to Davisons.

Thursday. February 5, 1863

Blustering & cold. I done all the chores this morning myself. Father went up to uncle Nathans. David Bothwell called at our house & we went over to the school house a visiting. It was very cold there. Romaine carried the children home from school. Helen King went up to Davisons tonight. Choped enough wood for night.

Friday, February 6, 1863

Stormy rain in the morning. Soon after snow, went

over to the shed & rode back with Brian. Wrote three letters. Uncle Harris called in on his way home. Went to burns to a party, had a very nice time. Got home about three o'clock, found a good fire. Quite stormy evening.

Saturday, February 7, 1863
Pleasant. Got up about ten o'clock, took breakfast about eleven. Went over to Burrs and had a very good visit. Played checkers with uncle Joe. Father carried mother, Augusta & I over & then went to Milan. Got back about dark & went after our folks. Daniel killed a beef.

Sunday, February 8, 1863
Pleasant. Read some in the morning. Harvey came up and got me. I had a very good time eating apples & cider & smoking. Talked over old times some. Elder Bouton & son come to Rubins. Had a very good visit with them. Come to meeting, sermon very good. Rode up with Dan.

Monday, February 9, 1863
Some stormy. Done some of the chores this morning, knit this forenoon. Father choped some afternoon. Went out to the woods with father to draw some wood. Last day of school. Went over & fed the sheep. Stoped to Davisons a little while. Helen King went down to Lons.

Tuesday, February 10, 1863
Cloudy & windy. Got up quite late, found uncle Joe at our house. Had quite a visit with him. Father went off to file his saw. I went down to Burrs a visiting. Read Meads letter. Come home after dark. Fatherwent over to Davisons tonight. Someone tried to fool some call. (?)

Wednesday, February 11, 1863

Pleasant. Done the chores this morning. Stoped to Burrs & got Scott. Father went to Ithica this morning with a load of wood. Choped some wood to last all night. Mary, Amelia, Thirsey & Prisp Seartes, aunt Keziah & Ida come here & stayed all night. Father got home about nine.

Thursday, February 12, 1863

Stormy. Snow very fast in morning. Hitched up & I, mother & Keziah went down to Rubins. Come home then went to Groton. Went up to the village called at the store then to Mrs Jacobs, then to the tavern, stayed a while, saw Hearvey & several others then to Keziahs.

Friday, February 13, 1863

Cloudy but pleasant with a little snow. Done some chores for Keziah, went to see Eugene, fetched them back home. Went down again, called to uncle Manleys then to Davids. Went to the store. Received a letter & valentines. Fetched pack a grist.

Saturday, February 14, 1863

Done some chores & knit in the forenoon. Father come down about two o'clock. Rode up town with Kiziah bought a few nick nacks. Come with father, David Lazelle rode up also. Stoped and fed the sheep, called at Davisons also a uncle Burris then home. Helped do some of the chores.

Sunday, February 15, 1863

Pleasant & warm. Shaved. Aunt Louise & uncle Nathan & Sheldon came down, had a nice time. Snow balled some. Went to Helen Davis in the afternoon & stayed in the evening. I went home with her, very bad walking. Fed the sheep at the shed. Felt very well, went to bed early.

Monday, February 16, 1863

Pleasant with a little snow. The folks shoveled out the roads. Pared some apples, knit som, hitched up the team & drawed two loads of wood. Put out the team and done some chores, to the barn. Mr. Davison in the evening & fetched me a letter from L. Davison.

Tuesday, February 17, 1863

Pleasant. Flora came over here for me to go after Amilia so I went over to Gengsis to get Amilia with rines horse and cutter. Wrote a letter to L. & Ezra. Went to Groton took mother & Amilia. Mother bought some dishes. Grandmother went to Mr. Brinsmaid spree Simons.

Wednesday, February 18, 1863

Pleasant. Grandma went over to Davisons & got his wife to go to Groton. Sheldon come and went to the spree with me. Had quite a number there. Had a jolly time. Went to bed about four o'clock. Played eucre some in the evening. Pained about half the night.

Thursday, February 19, 1863

Rainy all day. Mr. Dopson was here part of the day. I went over to uncle Burrs & called a spell, then to Davisons. The Cook girls & Mrs Trip was there. I went over to Briah Greenleaf & seen her knit some of the day. Went to bed quite early in the evening, slept very good, felt very well.

Friday, February 20, 1863

Very stormy, snow & wind. Father fetched over the gumper. I & mother & Augusta went up to uncle Nathans & made a visit. Played dominos some of the time. Come home about dark. Fetched down Wilbers, Bobs & Johns harness. Very blustering, put out the team. Father fixed the hopper some.

The cold winter days and nights of New York state, with the snow and wind, provided many hours in which people had to entertain themselves. Many parlor games were played, such as dominos, checkers, euchre and other card games. Andrew Gale tells of making his own homemade dominos. The men also knitted and crocheted for a pasttime. The snows began early in the winter and lasted well into the spring.

Saturday, February 21, 1863

Pleasant & cold. Knit in the forenoon, done the chores at noon, shoveled the snow out of the hen coop, went over to Davisons. They had company, Alan & wife & Emilines cousin. Stayed the afternoon. Lida Hicks was there also. Received a letter from Helen. Fed the sheep & went home.

Sunday, February 22, 1863

Cloudy & cold in the morning. Commenced snowing before noon & snowed all the rest of the day. Father went up to uncle Nathans. Done the chores at noon & the chores at night. Father fed the sheep. Had pudding & milk for supper. Felt quite well today.

Monday, February 23, 1863

Pleasant & warm. Sheldon came down for grandma to go up there & stay a spell. Pared some apples. Father went to the hollow. I done the chores at night. Called in to Davisons. I stayed a spell with Emmett. Rather poor news from Groton.

Tuesday, February 24, 1863

Pleasant. Got up early & took breakfast. Uncle Manley come up to our house early. I went to Rubin & father went to Milan. Looked out all day for strangers. George Ludlow come to Rubins & stayed a spell. Father come down & so did Daniel. Went to bed early. Daniel stayed all night.

Wednesday, February 25, 1863

Very pleasant. Harvey & I went down in the woods & sawed some wood. Come up at noon. Hariet Ludlow was there. Went back sawed in the afternoon. Come up & took supper then Harvey hitched up & went down to Ludlows. Come up be Bill Greenlick & fetched up Hoyt. Had a bully visit with him. Stayed to Rubins.

Thursday, February 26, 1863

Not very pleasant, rained some. Whittled & marked dominos. Phebe Jane come over to get a horse for old Husgal to go to mill. Harve & I took a ride in the afternoon. Rode until chore time. Heard from the Captain in the evening. A wedding to Brinsmaids in the evening. Stayed home.

Friday, February 27, 1863

Pleasant. Hitched up Gin to the buggy, went down to Rubins, got Harvey went down to Ludlows, from there to mits, then to uncle Hirams, from there to Milan then back again. Went to a donation with Fanny Rozette & Elen. Had a good time. Got back about five o'clock.

Saturday, February 28, 1863

Pleasant. Locked the girls in a room upstairs. Started for home bout nine, got home about ten. Went to be eleven, got up about five. Ate my supper & went to bed again. Helen Davison come over to our house in the afternoon, stayed in the evening. Got a letter from Ezra.

Sunday, March 1, 1863

Stormy, snowed most all day. Went to uncle Henry's to see Jay Gipe & boiss come over there with the stears. I went over to uncle Hirams about four o'clock, found the girls and Harvey there. Had a very good time carried on rather high. Harvey took Rozette home about dark.

Monday, March 2, 1863
Pleasant & warm. Come home with Daniel from Rubins. Wrote a letter to the Captain & one to uncle Ezra. Felt rather worse for ware. Sheldon come down to our house, father went to the hollow, mother & I went up to uncle Nathans. John Gilispie worked for father. Played dominos some in the evening.

Tuesday, March 3, 1863
Cloudy but not much storm. Felt rather down. Finished my thirteenth pair of socks this forenoon.. Mother washed, Grandma went down to Stephens Westcotts. I crossear some in the afternoon. Father went to Groton got a couple of pipes for me. Helen Davison come over here & fetched Augusta aline & co.

Wednesday, March 4, 1863
Pleasant but cold. Crossead some in the forenoon. Uncle Nathan & Aunt Louise went over to uncle Henrys. Sheldon, Flora & Stephen come down to our house & stayed. Father went and carried Tompsons & Kitte home. I done the chores, called at uncle Burrs to see Manley then Romaine & I went over to Davisons. Stayed the evening & visited with Theli & Helen. Felt rather down in the head.

Thursday, March 5, 1863
Very pleasant. Got a very bad cold. Harvey drawed a load of wood to the hollow. Father & I drawed a log from the woods. When Harvey come back, I rode home with him. I went to adonation at night. Carried Harriet Searlis. I stayed to Rubins all night. Aunt Louise come to our house & made a visit.

Friday, March 6, 1863

Pleasant but cloudy. Harvey got home about six o'clock. We hitched up the team and drawed some wood out to the road. After dinner we went out & split some wood at the door. About three he hitched up the colt and took me home. In the evening Harvey come to our house & we went up to Bothwells to a surprise in a load

Saturday, March 7, 1863

Stormy, snowed all day. Come down to the vender with Wilber & John. Played eucre with the boys some in the morning. Come to Rubins, stayed the rest of the day. They had visitors. Mr. & Mrs. Conklin & Mr. & Mrs Dates. Daniel Brinsmaid also father come to Rubins to. Felt pretty well in the evening.

Sunday, March 8, 1863

Stormy in the morning, clear up some about ten. Daniel, Mary & Rubin went to meeting in Milan. Went up home hitched up. Mother & I went over to uncle Henrys. She sat up with Jay. I went over to uncle Hirams. Jack come along while I was there. Hitched up and took James up to meeting, from there to uncle Henrys.

Monday, March 9, 1863

Pleasant with some wind. Got home about six o'clock. Harvey drawed some wood. I went over to Burrs in the morning, took dinner to Davisons. Father went to the hollow in the afternoon to get me to help him some. Felt rather down. Father seen Wilobey Major. Went to bed rather early.

Tuesday, March 10, 1863

Very pleasant. Knit some. Had company about noon. Iseral Knopp, his wife and four children come. Had a very good time.

Scott & the boys rode down hill most of the time. Harvey drawed wood to the hollow. He stoped to our house just at night. Father and I went to Milan in the evening. It snowed & Blowed some.

Wednesday, March 11, 1863

Very pleasant & warm. Loaded up a load of corn for father. He went to McGrawville with Breahs bobs. Fitch Kelly come to the Davisons. I done the chores when I went to the shed. I called at Burrs a spell then to Davisons. Harve come in the evening. Ciphered some until quite late. Harve stayed with me all night.

Thursday, March 12, 1863

Pleasant. Stayed at home most of the day. About two went down to Rubins found no one at home. Found the men folks down in the woods. Sawed some. Rubin went to the mill with a log. Our folks went to Groton. Come up to the house about dark, got supper. Harve went after his mother. I went home & back again

Friday, March 13, 1863

Pleasant but cold. Harve and I went down in the woods to saw some. The saw was dull & we come to the house. Harve mended his buffale robe. Riged up & started for the maskerade about three. I come home about five. Had all the chores to do & chop wood. Father got home about nine.

Saturday, March 14, 1863

Pleasant & cold. Done some of the chores. Father went off to Groton. Keziah & Ida & Rogers come to our house & made a visit. Harvey come to our house. I done the chores. Father come home about dusk. I went down home with Harvey afoot. Harve went to bed early. I pared apples for home.

Sunday, March 15, 1863

Pleasant. Harve hitched up in the morning & took Daniels harness home. I hitched up about noon & went down to Rubins, hitched to the cutter & Harve, John & I went to Ludlows. I got some cider. When I got home I found Elmire & Helen there. Uncle Stephen come here.

Monday, March 16, 1863

Pleasant most of the day. Snowed some in the morning. Went to Ithica, got there about noon. Got barbered, took dinner at Leons, went up town, got my likeness taken, hitched up the horses & come home. Bare ground part of the way. Got home about nine o'clock. Had the headache.

Tuesday, March 17, 1863

Pleasant. Ermira & Helen come over here in the forenoon. Choped some wood, sawed some in the afternoon. Daniel Wilson, Mary Sarakonn & Mary Darne come here and stayed the evening. Had a very good visit. Harvey and I went off about ten o'clock & took a ride. Went to bed about four o'clock. Snowed some in the night.

Wednesday, March 18, 1863

Pleasant. Fed the sheep, took breaffast to Rubins, Harve helped Donitz saw wood. Felt very well through the day. About dark went down to Rubins. I & Harve had to fix up & shore had a great time starting smoked coming. They were dancing when we got there. Had a very good time. Harve went home about three. I stayed with the girls.[20]

---

[20]This entry did not read as easily as most of the pages thus far. Might have been due to the condition Andrew was in after his all night ordeal.

Thursday, March 19, 1863

Pleasant. Got up about eight o'clock. Took breakfast & went to bed again. Had consederable fun. Got up about four o'clock & took supper & then went to bed again. Had some funny talk in the evening. Slept all night with my clothes on. Quite sleepy. James went to the hop..visited with Ellen.

Friday, March 20, 1863

Pleasant. Got up about seven o'clock, about the time James got home. James went to bed and slept a spell. Started for home about noon and got home about three o'clock. The girls come over with me. Fed the sheep & went to Groton Hollow. Went to uncle Steves. Uncle Nathan & aunt Louise come to our house & stayed the evening.

Saturday, March 21, 1863

Blowed & drifted considerable. Hitched up the team & took Rubins Faning mill home then went over to Wescotts. Come back & drew home a gag of hay. Went down to Groton in the afternoon with father. Saw aunt Suzy, Cora & William. Come home about dark. Harvey come here in the evening, stayed all night.

Sunday, March 22, 1863

Pleasant. Thawed very fast all day. Harve & I went over & fed the sheep. Went & bowed with Romain some. Sheldon, Flora, Stevey, aunt Louise, uncle Ratthorn come to our house. Harve stayed most all day. Uncle William & aunt Lucy come over here just at night. Mattered the horses & fed them oats.

Monday, March 23, 1863

Pleasant. Verna come down with the mumps. This morning uncle Nathan, Sheldon, Flora & Steve come down to our house. Father & I come down to Groton. I stayed down &

visited with Mrs Jacobs. Took dinner. Visited with Mary & Amitia in the afternoon, went uptown at night. Stayed all night at uncle Davids.

Tuesday, March 24, 1863

Pleasant. Took breakfast at uncle Davids. Aunt Melia & Mary come up there a visiting. Had a very good visit. Went downtown in the afternoon. Father come to Groton. Wrote a letter to Mead also one to Frank Smith. Helen, Wlmira & Mary wrote in my letter. Went to bed quite late.

Wednesday, March 25, 1863

Quite unpleasant with some rain. Went downtown, got my picture taken then went to Amelia & Marys room and stayed there all day. Elmina & Helen was to have company in the afternoon. Got home about dark I rode up with uncle Burr.

Thursday, March 26, 1863

Some stormy. Went down to Rubins. Harvey & John were choping. Mary was finishing her quilt. I took dinner there, played dominos in the afternoon & sing some. A peddler come there. Daniel come down about dark. Went down to Ludlows. The boys stayed at singing school. Hoyt was sick. Got home about ten. Father & mother gone.

Friday, March 27, 1863

Pleasant. Went over to Burrs before breakfast. Mary come over to our house. I took her to Rubins. I come back & father went down to Wescotts to get some hay. Uncle Harris come here and stayed a spell. I went down after Mary & stayed all night. They had a comforter on, slept rather poor. Wind blew.

Saturday, March 28, 1863

Snowed part of the day. Come home from Rubins about nine

o'clock. Stayed home most all day. Fed the sheep & stoped to Davisons a spell. Come home about dusk, took supper. Mary stayed the evening & I accompnayed her home. Got a kiss for the trouble.

Sunday, March 29, 1863

Snowed & blew all day. Stayed home all day, played dominos with Scott. Lay abed part of the day, shaved, had my neck washed & my hair oiled. Fed the sheep. Found the sheep all right but one u (ewe) had kicked the bucket. Father went over & picked u some & done the chores at dark.

Monday, March 30, 1863

Pleasant & warm. Cut some wood or sawed some. Daniel drew some stone for his house. Burr sawed wood with the log saw. Father went to Groton with a log. Uncle Harris & aunt Ruth come here today. They took the old sheep home. I done the chores at the barn. Father got home about dusk & fed the sheep.

Tuesday, March 31, 1863

Snowed all day long. Father drew some logs to the house for wood. Sawed some after dinner. Stayed around the house most of the time. Aunt Louise, Steve & Flora come here this afternoon. Father drew logs and Scott was with him. I fed the sheep, stoped where uncle Burr was sawing wood & then helped.

Wednesday, April 1, 1863

The snow blew very fast & hard in the forenoon. Pleasant in the afternoon, took a walk after dinner. Uncle Burr & aunt Thursa & children went to Simon Cooks today. Harvey called here today. He goes to a exibetion & takes Mrs Denoles at home this evening.

Thursday, April 2, 1863

Cloudy but pleasant. Wrote to Ezra. Took it over to Burrs. John Sharpstein & Eck come there while I was there. Went up in the lot with the team & helped father. Helped him some in the afternoon. Come upearly, fed the sheep, went over to Burrs in the evening, played dominos & went home with a girl.

Friday, April 3, 1863

Pleasant & warm. Went up in the sugar bush taped some trees in the forenoon. In the afternoon went down where uncly Burr was boiling sap. Ann Champlain, her mother & Mrs Bosworth come to our house a visiting. Got home just as the children were eating. Helen Davison was here. I went down to Rubins. Harve was not at home.

Saturday, April 4, 1863

Pleasant & warm. Helped father take the log saw up in the lot. Augusta & Laverna went over to Davisons, a visiting. Father received a letter from Ezra. So did John Sharpstein. His was rather billious. Stayed at home in the evening. Felt very well, went to bed early.

Sunday, April 5, 1863

Stormy most all day. Shaved, went up to aunt Louises, played dominos a spell, had some warm sugar. Amos & Wilber called in a spell. Went down with Wib from there to our house & then to meeting. Preaching by old Broughton. Not a very heavy congregation, a good sermon.

.

As spring neared and the weather began turning warmer, more outside activities could be enjoyed and Andrew took advantage of this to practice his markmanship. Hearing about word from his Uncle Ezra, he might have begun thinking about Army life again.

Warmer weather also meant it was time to begin the spring

chores on the farm such as plowing, clearing fields and sowing crops. It was to assist his father, in these labors, that kept Andrew home for almost six months, instead of on the battlefieds of the South.

Monday, April 6, 1863
Pleasant & warm. Went over to Davisons. Uncle Steve come along, I rode home with him. After dinner shot a mark till about four o'clock then he went home. I rode over & fed the sheep. Stoped to Davisons, stayed a spell, come home, took supper, went to bed early.

Tuesday, April, 7, 1863
Stormy with snow. Town meeting. Father went to Groton. I, Scott, Gusta, & mother went to uncle Nathans not far from noon. Come home, went over to Burrs, stayed until most of the night. Stoped to Davisons, then home. Feel very well. Fed the sheep & co(w).

Wednesday, April 8, 1863
Pleasant part of the day & part of the day stormy. Fed the sheep in the morning. Father got his horses shod in the forenoon. In the afternoon sawed some logs. Come to the house, done the chores alone. John Sharpstein come here in the afternoon. Sung some in the evening.

Thursday, April 9, 1863
Pleasant & warm. Drew logs all day. Aunt Louise come down here in the morning, got Grandmother, left Flora here. Sheldon come down & fetched Grandma home. Uncle Burr took father up at his on price for his farm. Done some of the chores at night. Received a letter from Ezra.

Friday, April 10, 1863
Pleasant. Went over to Burrs, got 18 tin pans then went to

the sap bush. Boiled some in the forenoon, went out in the afternoon, filled up the kettle. It commenced raining. Come to the house. Went over to Davisons, stayed a spell, fed the sheep & done the chores alone. Went up in the lot.

Saturday, April 11, 1863
Pleasant most of the day. Went up to the sap bush, drew up some logs, boiled all day. Father helped me some. John Sharpstein come up in the bush where we were. Come up to the house, done the chores. Stoped to Davisons. Emeline come home. Went up to the wood & helped fetch horse. Stayed all night with me up the surap.

Sunday, April 12, 1863
Pleasant. Harve & I sawed wood this morning before breakfast. Took breakfast. Harvey & I went over to Davisons a spell then to Burrs & eat butternuts then come home & sung a spell. Went out & done some of the chores. Come in & sit a spell & went to bed.

Monday, April 13,1863
Pleasant with a cool north wind. Went home with Harve in the morning. Choped & split & piled wood in the forenoon. In the afternoon, went down in Howards sap bush, then to the house, then down in the lot. Come up about six o'clock. Took supper then come home & done the chores. Called to Davisons & Burrs.

Tuesday, April 14, 1863
Pleasant & warm. Fed the sheep. Called to Davisons, sent a letter down to Groton by Mr. Davison & some tobaco. Went up in the lot to see about the sap. Come down about noon. After dinner went down in Burrs sap bush then to ours. Come down about six o"clock. Went over to the shed. Received two

letters tonight.

Wednesday, April 15, 1863

Pleasant. Father quite unwell. I went up in the sapbush & boiled until noon. Come down found uncle Steven, Keziah, Ida & uncle Nathan. Shot a mark until about four o'clock then went up in the sapbush, suruped off. Come down, fed the sheep, stoped to uncle Burrs. Went down in the bush with him.

Thursday, April 16, 1863

Rather stormy all day. Fixed up and went up to uncle Nathans & played dominos with Sheldon until four o'clock. Started for home, stoped to Sharpsteins & to Brinsmaids. Fed the sheep. Stoped to Daniels a spell. Augusta come down with the mumps. Went over to Burrs in the evening.

Friday, April 17, 1863

Some lousy. Went over to Davisons, stayed until almost noon. Come home & shot at a mark twice & missed the mark twice. Went over to Burrs. Romain was plowing, Burr was sifting grass seed. Fed the sheep, went over to home, then come back to Davisons & played dominos with Romain.

Saturday, April 18, 1863

Pleasant. Put up a grist. Went down to Rubins. Harve was plowing. Hoyt come up & stayed as long as I did. I come home about five. Father went to Groton. I done the chores. Helen come over to our house. I come home with her & stayed the evening. Romain was there.

Sunday, April 19, 1863

Pleasant & warm. Shaved & washed up. Hitched up & went down to Rubins to go to meeting.[21] Took a ride, got back as Rubins folks were eating supper. Took another ride. Went to uncle Hirams. Got home about two o'clock.

Monday, April 20, 1863

Rather stormy part of the day. Went over to Burrs in the forenoon. I got up about eleven. H Cain worked for Burr part of the day. I went down on the creek after a load of hay. Got some wet. Fed the sheep. Stoped to Davisons & read the news. Got home about nine.

Tuesday, April 21, 1863

Pleasant & warm. Watered the horses & fed them. Went over to Davisons & played dominos with John Gilispie. After dinner went up in the lot. John split three rails & left all of a sudden. I helped father draw stone. Come down & done the chores. Stoped to Davisons a spell. Burr seems some woried.

Wednesday, April 22, 1863

Pleasant & warm. Fetched some water for mother to wash. Went up in the lot & uncovered a potato hole & plowed some in the forenoon. Plowed all the afternoon. Traded watch chains twice, fed the sheep, stoped to Davisons, received a letter from Ezra.

Through out the diary, both while at home on the farm and later, after returning to duty, Andrew mentioned his health as not being very good. In this next entry, he starts out with "Not very well". This phrase is used many times during his writings.

---

[21] Here the diary had two lines of some sort of code. Dots in boxes

Thursday, April 23, 1863

Pleasant & warm. Not very well. Went up to uncle Nathans, got a hart from Helen Brown. Went out in the woods where Sheldon was. Played dominos all the afternoon with Sheldon. Come home after dark. Stoped to Davisons. Phebe was at home, talked with her in the evening.

Friday, April 24, 1863 *****

Lousy. I looked over some fotos in the forenoon. Went over to Davisons, from there down in the woods where Romain was. Come home then to Davisons. Phebe went home about five o'clock. Went over where Romain was plowing. Done all the chores. Received to letters. Harve went to Groton. Andrew H. Gale's birthday.*****

Saturday, April 25, 1863

Pleasant. Wrote two letters this morning. Took them over to Mr. Davisons, he took them to Groton. Gathered the sap things. Went up to uncle Nathans & got my hair cut & played dominos with Flora & Sheldon. Holden stoped to Nathans. I took a walk quite a piece in the evening.

Sunday, April 26, 1863

Pleasant & a cool wind. Fixed up and went to Rubins & went to meeting with them & drove the team. Harve wacked down a fool. Come home, hitched up and took a ride. Went to singing school & up to Searles a spell. Emitine Davisons birthday.

Monday, April 27, 1863

Pleasant & quite cool. Went up in the lot & plowed in the forenoon. Finished to plowing up north of stubble. Commenced plowing up south. Plowed until supper time. Went over to Davisons then to Burrs. Stayed quite a spell.

Burr set fire to some brush heeps.

Tuesday, April 28, 1863
Pleasant & warm. Helped clean the celler in the forenoon. Picked up some pototoes after dinner. Then Miss Gale Manley & Eddie Green come over here a visiting. Helen come home in the afternoon. I took a walk in the evening.

Wednesday, April 29, 1863
Pleasant & warm. Sorted over potatoes in the forenoon. In the afternoon I went up in the lot then come home then to Burrs. Come home about dark & choped some wood & done the chores. Helen stayed all night with Gusta.

Thursday, April 30, 1863
Pleasant & warm. Grandma went up to aunt Louises a visiting. Aunt Mary & Amelia worked for mother in the afternoon. I hitched up the pony & drove hime down to Rubins. Went down where Harve was a draging. Drove home & done the chores.

Chapter Four

The beginning of May found Andrew Gale still at home on the farm near Groton, New York. He continued assisting his father with the spring work in the fields and around the farm. Plowing, planting, wood chopping, dragging logs, and other labors, and chores, were there to do and Andrew did them.

Friday, May 1, 1863
Pleasant. Hitched up & plowed all the forenoon. Mary & Amelia was to our house, sewed for mother. Draged in the ahternoon until four o'clock then Davison come over & sewed the wheat. I worked until quite dark, put out the team, very tired indeed.

Saturday, May 2, 1863
Warm & pleasant. Commenced draging before eight. Mr Davison come over & sowed the grass seed for Grandma. Father went down to Groton in the afternoon. I went over where Daniel was plowing & then to Davisons. Father got home after dark.

Sunday, May 3, 1863
Pleasant & warm. Went over to Davisons. Went home, fixed up & drove down to Rubins. Harve was alone. Come up to meeting, went off with John Sharpstein to Tirea, from there to Groton, then around out home. Got home about ten o'clock.

Monday, May 4, 1863
Stormy, rained quite hard most of the forenoon. Run the buggy out to soak. To dinner over to Davisons a spell, come back & washed my buggy. Picked some greens with Romaine & Davison, went over to Burrs, sucked four eggs.

Tuesday, May 5, 1863

Quite pleasant in the forenoon. Hitched up pony, went to uncle Henrys. Got the pony shod & bought a whip. After dinner sowed grass seed for Eck, took supper to uncle Henrys. Come home in the rain. Got my buggy all muddy.

Wednesday, May 6, 1863

Very unpleasant. Snowed quite hard in the morning. Soon turned to rain. Went over to Burrs & duned (?) for some. Went home, went to Burrs with Harve then home, from there to Rubins. Stayed there afternoon & stayed all night.

Thursday, May 7, 1863

Quite stormy. Rained most of the day. Looked over reins most of the forenoon, went down in the lot with Harve to plow. Come home, then to Davisons. Stayed until evening. Uncle Joe come there. Father went to Groton.

Friday, May 8, 1863

Pleasant & warm. Drew a jag of hay, then went up in the lot. Drew some rails & fooled around until noon. Carried a trough up in the lot then come down & got the horses. Drew a load of rails & washed the sheep. Plowed some and done the chores.

Saturday, May 9, 1863

Pleasant & warm. Went over to Burrs & layed around all the forenoon. Father went to Groton. I plowed in the afternoon. Aunt Louise come to our house, took supper at five. I went over to Davisons in the evening. Father got home about nine.

Sunday, May 10, 1863

Pleasant & warm. Shaved & fixed up in the afternoon, After

dinner hitched up the pony & started. Got a little ways, met Hoyt & Brown & come back. Then went over to Hirams. Come back about dark. The news come that old Jeff was taken.

Monday, May 11, 1863

Pleasant & warm. Went over to the school house. Come home with Helen. Helped mother clean out the cellar. Took some butter over to holaday, got back about dark. Went over to Davisons in the evening. Stayed quite late.

Tuesday, May 12, 1863

Pleasant & warm. Went over to Davisons then come home & went down to uncle Stephens. Stayed a spell, got home about five. Nathan helped Daniel drag. Went up to Perkinsons with Romaine. Come back & called to Davisons.

As evidenced in the diary, Andrew Gale was not a lazy person and he seemed to be recovering quite well from whatever illness it was that sent him to the hospital and then home from the war. He continued working hard for his father, as well as playing hard with his friends and relatives.

There were days, however, when he would still complain of not feeling well and this went on even when he reported back to his regiment, later.

It is not known just how large Peter Gale's farm was. The 1860 Federal Census[22] listed the value of the Real Estate at $1000. Whatever the size, Andrew states that he planted corn, potatos, (potatoes as he called them), and wheat as part of their crops. The plowing and planting took almost two months to complete, using

---

[2]DeWitt County N. Y. Historical Society

horse drawn plows.

Wednesday, May 13, 1863

Cloudy. Shelled half a bushel of corn to plant. George Ludlow come here about noon. He helped me plant corn. I went over to get Burrs help but he could not help. After we got through we went over to Davisons.

Thursday, May 14, 1863

Rainy. Planted in the forenoon & father plowed it some before dinner. Finished planting. It rained so as to stop work. Went up to Burrs then to Perkinsons, then to Davisons, then home then back to Davisons, then home & to bed

Friday, May 15, 1863

Pleasant & windy. Spread some manure and planted some potatoes in the garden & wrote some letters. Went up in the lot where Romain was plowing then to the house. Hitched up went to Holidays, then to Groton, then home.

Saturday, May 16, 1863

Pleasant but cloudy. Stayed at home in the forenoon. Helen come to out house. I went over to Burrs, went up in the lot with Romain & stayed a spell then come home & choped some wood. Went down to Groton. It rained. Harvey & Romain stayed all night.

Sunday, May 17, 1863

Pleasant & quite cold. Fixed up, went down to Rubins. Harve hitched up the team for Rubin. He went to meeting a foot. We rode up to Nathans & found Johnathen. Went to singing school from there up on the hill then oph....

Monday, May 18, 1863

Cloudy & Cold. School commenced. I draged in the forenoon. Romain plowed. When Romain come down I rode to Burrs. Thissy got her history of this war. Come down home & went to bed.

Tuesday, May 19, 1863

Pleasant & cool. Drew manure & manured the corn in the forenoon on the hill. Planted some in the afternoon. Rode up with Romain, smoked with him. Helen come to our house. Feel rather under the weather.

Wednesday, May 20, 1863

Pleasant & warm. Planted some corn & Benn Hatch come up here & stayed quite a spell. Grandma & Mrs Davison went down to Steven Wescott a visiting. Hitched up the pony & went to Rubins.

Thursday, May 21, 1863

Pleasant & warm. Felt rather poorly. Went up to Reskins & traded chains. Come home, went to Rubins. Washed my buggy, come home & fixed up & took a ride & took Harve. Got home about eleven.

Friday, May 22, 1863

Pleasant & warm. Run around in the forenoon. In the afternoon I plowed some. James Wallace come to our house. I took him to Milan. Aunt Louise come to our house & made a visit. I got home from Milan at dark.

Saturday, May 23, 1863

Pleasant & warm. Father sowed some corn in the forenoon. In the afternoon he went to Groton. I planted some potatoes, went over to Burrs & stayed a spell. Then come over to Davisons, then home.

Sunday, May 24, 1863

Pleasant & warm. I shaved. Romain come over here, so did Davison. We went down to the creek, got back about three. Went to meeting, come home, hitched up the pony & took a ride around. Got home about eleven.

Monday, May 25, 1863

Cloudy & cool. Libby Perkins called here & wanted me to help their folks plant corn. Come home after got through, then went down to Rubins then down to drink, then home. Went over to Burrs & to Davisons & home & to bed.

With most of the planting and field work completed by the latter part of May, tasks of different natures needed to be taken care of. Fences required mending, the buggy was to bevarnished, there was plastering work to be done and wood to be gathered for the kitchen. All of this fell to Andrew to do. There was no word or thought, yet, of reporting back to his Army duties.

Tuesday, May 26, 1863

Cloudy & cool. Went up to Perkins a little while. Come home and drew some rails & fixed some fence, then hitched up & went to Milan & got some varnish to varnish the buggy. Uncle Harris & wife come to our house.

Wednesday, May 27, 1863

Pleasant & warm. Went to the stone mill for some plaster. Got there about eleven. Got loaded about three, got home about sundown. Went over to Burrs, stayed a spell, then to Davisons, then home.

Thursday, May 28, 1863

Pleasant & warm. Fixed up to go to Auburn but made up my mind not to go. Nathan worked for Grandma. Went to

Groton & went to uncle Davids. From there to uncle Harris Bostwicks. From there home. Took a walk.

There came days, when the chores were all completed or could be postponed until later, and on one such day, Andrew made a trip to the town of Auburn. He stayed there for two days visiting and getting his picture taken.

Friday, May 29, 1863
Pleasant & warm. Started for Auburn. Got there about eleven o'clock. Went down town after dinner, had my photograph taken, got my watch fixed, went up to tea. Went down town again. Went to the semetry. Got back about ten.

Saturday, May 30, 1863
Pleasant & warm. Went down town a spell. Went to the prison. Got my photographs. I got my horse & started for Flemming. Got there about eleven. They had visitors in the afternoon. Started for home about ten.

Sunday, May 31, 1863
Pleasant & warm. Took a ride over on the hill to meeting, then to Hirams, then to meeting, then back, then to Groton. Stayed a spell. Rained some. Got home about nine. Pretty mad. Put out the horse & went to bed.

Monday, June 1, 1863
Rather dull weather.

Tuesday, June 2, 1863
(No Entry)

Wednesday, June 3, 1863
Rather unpleasant in the morning. Went up to Nathans &

drew manure. Got home about two o'clock. Went over to Davisons. After supper, took a scoot out & got some wedding cake.

For unknown reasons, Andrew made no entries into his diary for the next four days but began reentering the details, beginning on Sunday, June 7. His social life increased somewhat the next few days, as did some of the other work around the farm, like sheep shearing and road repairing.

Thursday, June 4, 1863

(No Entry)

Friday, June 5, 1863

(No Entry)

Saturday, June 6, 1863

(No Entry)

Sunday, June 7 1863

Cool & with some rain. Fanny came to our house, had a good visit. I took her down to Howards. Aunt Loiuse, uncle Nathan, Flora, Sheldon's stepson here about four o'clock.

Monday, June 8, 1863

(No Entry)

Tuesday, June 9, 1863

Pleasant & warm. Went up to Bothwells after Frank, then took Helen & Miss Wallace to uncle Nathans & stayed the evening & played dominos. Took a ride, met Jack, got home about one o'clock.

Wednesday, June 10, 1863

Pleasant & warm. Sheared sheep all day, at night hitched up and took the Miss Wallace down to the corners, got home about one o'clock. Received a letter from uncle Ezra.

Thursday, June 11, 1863
Pleasant & warm in the morning. Worked on the road, took dinner to uncle Nathan. It rained about five o'clock.

Friday, June 12, 1863
Visited the school. Took the teacher home. Rained shortly after I got home.

Saturday, June 13,
(No Entry)

Sunday, June 14, 1863
Took a ride over to uncle Hirams, then fetched Miss Wallace on the hill.

Monday, June 15, 1863
(No Entry)

Tuesday, June 16, 1863
(No Entry)

Wednesday, June 17, 1863
(No Entry)

Thursday, June 18, 1863
(No Entry)

Again, there was a period of five or six days when Andrew Gale failed to record the day's events in his diary. One entry mentioned receiving a letter from his Uncle Ezra, a member of the 137th

Regiment. Something in that letter might have started Andrew thinking about his return to the regiment. When he does pick up the action, it was to relate his association with the school "marm". She seemed to be the one to whom he holds the warmest intentions.

Friday, June 19, 1863
Pleasant & warm. Took the school marm over to uncle Hirams. Stayed there all night.

Saturday, June 20, 1863
Pleasant. Took breakfast at Hirams. Played eucre all the forenoon. Took a ride at night and come home about twelve o'clock.

Sunday, June 21, 1863
Pleasant. Went to uncle Nathans. Come down & went to meeting with emeline. After meeting, took a ride over on east hill.

For the entire first six months of 1863, Andrew has made no mention of the war or of any of his attachments to the 137th Regiment. He had led the life of an average ordinary civilian citizen, but in the back of his mind, at all times, must have been the thought, that soon he would have to live up to his obligation to the Army, and return to his Company K and to the perils and sorrow of the war.

On June 22nd, as recorded in the diary, Andrew began his treck, back to army life. The diary, and letters that are included, record his attempt to rejoin the regiment.

Monday, June 22, 1863
Pleasant most of the day. Visited around in the forenoon, in the afternoon went to Ithica. Took the six o'clock train, arrived at Oswego at half past eight. Took the next train, got to Elmira at 11 o'clock, stayed till four.

Tuesday, June 23, 1863

Pleasant. Took the four o'clock train. Took breakfast in Williamsport, got to Harrisburg about noon, got to Baltimore about four, took supper. Took the eight o'clock train for Washington. Arrived in the city about ten.

Wednesday, June 24, 1863

Got up about six o'clock, pleasant all day. Took breakfast at the Arlington House. Run around town all day. Write three letters. Some rebel prisoners come to town just at night. Stayed at the Arlington House all night.

One of the letters, mentioned in the diary entry of June 24, was written to Andrew's family at home in Groton, N.Y It was saved and reads as follows.

Washington, June 24/63

Dear Parents.

As it was your request for me to write often, I seat myself in the barroom at the Arlington House to let you know how I prosper. I got to this place last night about ten o'clock. It is now noon. They are eating dinner. I am not hungry so I thought I would improve my time by writing. If I was at home I should try to eat some but I shall have to do as the ant told the cricket. If I live without work I must live without food. At least when I am not hungry. I have wrote a letter to Frank Smith. I am going to write one to uncle Ezra today. I have been to the Provost Marshels Office & to Gen. somebody's office, for I have forgotten his name, & no pass yet & I don't know when I can get one but I hope I shall soon. The army has moved. I guess it would have been a good plan for me to of stayed at home another week. Mother must not worry about me for I shall come out all right yet. No more at present.

From your son Andrew

Thursday, June 25, 1863

Pleasant but cool. Went up to General Krenselmans headquarters. Tried to get a pass but could not. Run around all day. Got pretty tight just at night. Went to the varieties.

Friday, June 26, 1863

Rather lousy in Washington. Took the eleven o clock train for Baltimore then took the three o'clock train for Harrisburg, three oclock for Elmira, got [23]

Saturday, June 27, 1863

Pleasant. Got to Elmira at twelve o'clock. Took a freight train for Oswego. From there took the three o'clock train to Ithica. Got there about six o'clock. Started for home afoot, got a ride five miles, stayed Louis'

Sunday, June 28, 1863

Pleasant. Took breakfast to uncle Nathans. Come down home about ten.

While Andrew Gale was in Washington, attempting to secure a pass, and reach his regiment, that same regiment, the 137th Regiment, N.Y.S.V. was beginning a move to the north, to stay between the Confederate Army, also moving north, and the city of Washington. The quirk of fate, that sent Andrew back home to Groton, kept him from joining the regiment and participating in the Battle of Gettysburg, just a few short weeks away. At that battle, July 1,2, & 3 the 137th Regiment suffered numerous casualties, while defending Culps Hill.[24]

---

[23] Andrew stopped here but continued his thought on the next day's entry

[24] 137th Regiment, N.Y.S.V. Regimental Records micro film

About the same time Andrew was arriving back in Groton, his Uncle Ezra wrote him a letter from the regiment, with news of the war and what was happening to them. It appeared that Andrew's absence from the regiment was beginning to raise some questions and it was Ezra's concern that he return as soon as possible, to prevent his getting into trouble with the Captain.

Ezra also held some concern that the Rebels were heading North and he issued a warning to the people of New York State to prepare for them.

Marland   June th29/63

Dear Nephew

I thought I wood writ you a few lines to let you know where I was and how I was get a long. I am midlin well fore considern the hard marches that we have had and I hope these few lines will find you well. I herd you was comin back but I am a feared it will bother you some to get back. Major wiley is sick and you can go down and se his folk and se where he is. I guess he is to Washington. If he is his folks wood know. He cod help you about a pass. We ur encamp in about a mile from Fredericksburg. Silly but how long we will stay I do not know. The Rebs ar workin this way. Tell the folks up that way they best be fickin up there old guns for the Rebs talk of comin down there. I don't think there is much fare play about this war. I had a talk with the Captain the other day and he wants you to get back here by the next month if you can. He said he had put it off as long as he dar. You had better get back here if you can by the first of August if you can. We left Verginia the 26 and crossed over Goos Crick toewards ferry the 28th. Ancer this as soon as you can. This is from your uncle Ezra. I am tired and can't writ much this tim. E

Monday, June 29, 1863

(No Entry)

Tuesday, June 30, 1863

(No Entry)

These were the events as they occurred up until the end of June of 1863, in the life of Andrew H. Gale. He had enlisted in the 137th Regiment, N.Y.S.V. in August of 1862 and was mustered into service, with them, on September 27th. They were sent to Virginia and were involved in a number of actions, almost immediately.

In December, he was sent to the hospital, due to illness, and then traveled home to Groton, New York, and he was still there on June 30, 1863.

The regimental records, reported in earlier pages, four versions in all, related what had transpired for the rest of the men, up until the end of June. Their service was already filled with heavy skirmishing and picket duty. Company K. and the 137th Regiment were battlefield veterans.

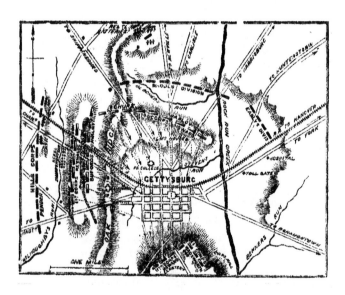

Chapter Five

The 137th Regiment, N.Y.S.V. monthly Rolls pick up the activities for the second half of 1863. The records begin on the first dauy of July.

> July 63   On the first day of July, left Littlestown, Pa. And marched about 18 miles on the Gettysburg turnpike beyond two taverens then filed left into a cornfield and formed in lines of battle. Sent out two companies of skirmishers then marched by flank through a small piece of woods into a wheatfield where we lay upon arms all night.
> July 2.   Marched about one mile to the right and took position at about the center of the right wing of the army. Commenced the construction of breast works which we completed about two oclock.[25] Waited until about 6:00 o'clock when we were ordered to change positions. Did so and took position to the right behind breast works erected and just previously occupied by the 2nd Brigade. Immediately upon our occupying of this position, the enemy opened a heavy fire upon

---

[5]This location, on the Gettysburg Battlefield, is known as Culps Hill

us and during the night flanked us upon the right driving us from our breast works with some considerable loss. We again rallied and charged upon the enemy driving them out from our defences. We then held out position that night.

Aftermath of the first two days of fighting at Gettysburg

This battle, of July 2nd, was a very important one for the Federal forces. Had the Confederate Units been able to capture and hold Culp's Hill, they would have controlled the right flank of the Union line and have driven the remaining Northern troops from their positions on the high grounds around Gettttsburg.

According to many accounts of the Battles at Gettysburg, the Southern Army missed a great opportunity by not occupying Culp's Hill on the afternoon of July 1, when it was unoccupied. According to information obtained, after the war, from Lieutenant General Richard S. Ewell, Commanding Officer of the Second Corps, of the Southern forces, that his corps of twenty thousand men, was in position to attack and was ready to move on Culp's Hill.[26] This was at 4:00 P. M. on the afternoon of July 1st. At that time he received orders from General Lee, directing him not to advance, but to take a defensive position.

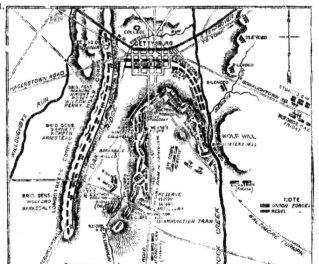

---

[26]"Reports and Letters of Lieutenant General Richard S. Ewell, CSA"

Again from the regimental records: The next day,

July 3rd and night July 4th. The enemy apparently having withdrawn, stacked arms, buried the dead, gathered in the wounded. Got some of our own and the enemy arms and rested.

July 5. Lay in the position doing some duties until about noon when we marched for Littlestown, Pa. We arrived in the afternoon,

July 7th. Remained in camp at Littlestown awaiting orders.

From the Field and Staff Muster Roll, the accounts of July and August are recorded and follow:

July & Aug. 1863 Kempers Ford   Aug. 31, 1863

Left Littlestown, Pa. July 1. Marched to Gettysburg to a position on the left of the line. Rested on our arms in line of battle until the morning of the 2nd when we shifted to the right of the line into a piece of woods (Culp's Hill) & there through up a breast work in front of our position. About 6 P. M. we were attacked by Ewell's Corps (CSA) and a heavy fire of musketry was kept up on both sides until about 10 o'clock after which the firing ceased, though renewed at intervals through the night. At 4 A. M. of the 3rd the enemy again advanced to the assult but were repulsed. A heavy fire of musketry was kept up until 10 1/2 A. M. when the enemy retired leaving many dead & wounded in front of our lines. Our loss was heavy being 4 officers killed and 3 wounded. 36 enlisted men killed & 86 wounded. During the firing, a white flag was raised by the enemy when about 70 came over the works and gave themseelves up as prisoners to the Regt.

Headquarters of Gen. George G. Meade, Gettysburg Battlefield

A third account of the first five days of July, 1863, comes from the records of Company K, 137th Regiment, and recorded by J. Walker:

July & Aug. 1863. Kempers Ford, Va. The night of the 1st of July we arrived on the battlefield of Gettysburg-formed in line of battle and lay on our arms over night. The 2nd, changed position so that we lay on the right of the center and then with the rest of this command, through up entrenchments. Nothing worthy of notice transpired until evening when we were warned of the approach of the enemy by the fire from the skirmish line-we had scarcely gained our position when they were driven(Skirmishers) in, closely followed by the enemy who attacked us furiously with superior numbers. After severe fighting, they were repulsed with a great loss in killed and wounded, after which, aided by superior numbers and the darkness of night, they succeeded in turning our flank. Our position was then changed and we held them in check until the fighting ceased. The following morning we were again attacked, but repulsed every attack of the enemy. About 10 o'clock A. M. a flag of truse was discovered in front of this command. The order was given to cease firing when of the enemy came in and gave themselves up as prisoners of war. Their position was such that it was death for them to advance or retreat. The fourth was spent in burying the dead. Our time since has been employed in following the enemy. We are now doing picket duty, drilling at this ford.

During these fateful days, for the 137th Regiment, in Gettysburg, Pa., Andrew Gale was back in Groton, New York after his attempt to get a pass to rejoin his Regiment, just a few weeks prior. His diary held no entries for the dates of July 1st or 2nd. He began his account on the 3rd.

Wednesday, July 1, 1863
(No Entry)

Thursday, July 2, 1863
(No Entry)

Friday, July 3, 1863
Pleasant & warm. Stayed around home most of the day.
Went down to Moravia to a dance.

Saturday, July 4, 1863
Some lousy through today. Got home about five in the
morning, went to bed, slept until noon then went up to uncle
Nathans & went a hunting with uncle Stephen.

Sunday, July 5, 1863
(No Entry)

A second letter was received, by Andrew, from his Uncle Ezra,
while he was still at home in Groton. This letter contains a vivid
description of some of the fighting that took place between the Union
and Confederate forces. Although Ezra did not specifically mentioned
Gettysburg, he says "We have been all over verginia and mylaind[27] and
pa[28] and back to harpers ferry". The letter is dated July 6, 1863, just
three days after the Battle of Gettysburg and if there were news
reports about the battle, Andrew could assume that his Uncle Ezra and
the "boys" had been there and had been involved. By Ezra's two
letters, it is easy to see that he was not as well educated as was

---

[7]Virginia and Maryland

[8]Pennsylvania

Andrew and Andrew's father, Peter Gale. These two letters were copied just as they were written, without editing.

Ezra Bostwick letter of July 16, 1863

Myrland July 16th/63

Dear Nephew

I received the 10th of July. I was very glad tohear from you. I was sorry to hear you had such bad luck. I look for you here every day till I got your letter. You started in a bad time to get here. There is a good meney things I wood like to writ but know time now we are on a march all of the time. We have been on a march 28 days and I have ben a nuther battle cince I rot to you last. You most see the it in some paper and so it be know yous of writen a bout it. I was in the fight 2 days.The first day it commences at 4 oclock in the afternoon and lased till 10 o nite and the rebs then fell back till 4 oclock AM and com a gun and they fussed till 12 oclock. I fired 100 and 60 rounds. I had a good meney close calls, there was a good meney of our bois kild & woned. There was a good meney fell around me. There was wone bulet went through my blanet that was rold up un my napsack. We have been all over verginia and mylaind and "pa" and back to harpers ferry. We are in campt in Plesent Valey in a mile of the old camp ground where we was wen you was here. We come here today. How long we will stay i do not know. I wood like to se you very much. I som times fell quite lomsom. Our comey[29] is quite small, There is 28 of us left here.I have seen John Davison and cene the battle and John ludlow that got through. Andrew Heth was kill and Biley Brown. We have drove the Rebs back in Verginia again. If we showd stay here long it wood be a good tim for you to come back to your comey. If you can see Major Wilbe he cou help you. Aberryh a brass he most be to Washington yet. If we shoo stay here I do not know if you wood heft to go there to get

---

[9]Company K

here. I se the Captain and he wants you to get here this month if cod. He said he putit of as long as he dar. I am well and hope these few lines will find you all well.

This is from your uncle Ezra

Cence I commence this letter I herd we was goin to stay here till we get our pay. If we do we will stay here quit a while. You heft to com back son or leave there. It might do to stay there. I se the Captain and hav him put it off as long as I can. Writ son as you get this.

When Andrew had made his first trip to Washington, in June, to get a pass from his Major for his return to the regiment, he was not successful and it is unknown what he learned at that time. On July 12, he began another attempt to get the proper papers to enable him to rejoin his comrads in the 137th Regiment, N.Y.S.V. This trip took him back to Washington, D. C., for a second time and he got there by another lengthy train ride, but this time he went by a different route than he had taken in June.

Upon his arrival in Washington, Andrew was able to locate the Major and get the credentials needed. He did, however, manage to remain in Washington for four days before leaving to locate his regiment. Pages containing Dates July 6-July 11, were missing from the diary.

Sunday, July 12, 1863

Pleasant & warm. Stayed around home most all day. Started for Auburn about eleven oclock. Got there about four in the morning.

Monday, July 13, 1863

Some lousy. Started for New York at half past eight. Arrived at New York at nine oclock. Stayed in the city until half past eleven. Quite a good deal of excitement in the city. Started for Washington at half past eleven.

Tuesday, July 14, 1863

Somewhat stormy. Had to wait a good while in the road on account of freshes. Got to Washington about 8 P M found the Maj. Stayed at the same house. Went to the varieties got in about eleven.

Wednesday, July 15, 1863

Not very pleasant. Got up at half past six, took breakfast an hour later. Stayed around the city all day.

Thursday, July 16, 1863

Pleasant & warm. Still in Washington not feeling very well. Stormed very hard at night.

Friday, July 17, 1863

Pleasant with some rain. Went to the canterbery tonight.

While Andrew Gale was in Washington, the following information was recorded in the three Regimental Records referred to in previous chapters.

Regimental Clerks Records, 137th Regiment, N.Y.S.V.

July 7th. Marched to near Frederick, Md

July 8th. Marched to near Jeffersonville, Md.

July 9th. Marched to near Rhorosville, Md.

July 10th. Marched to near the field of Antediam

July 11th. Marched to near Fairfax where being in the vicinity of the enemy we erected good and substantial breast works.

July 12th. Occupied the same position

July 13th. Occupied the same position until near night then marched about one mile and bivouwacked.

July 14th. Marched about two miles to the right before daylight near Jones Cross road. Here we erected stone breastworks and lay all night.

July 15th. Marched to near Harpers Ferry, Va.

July 16th. Marched to Pleasant Valley, Md. and encamped.

July 17th. Pleasant Valley

July 18th. The same.

In the Field & Staff Muster Roll it states the following:

Left Gettysburg July 6th & marched by way of Littlestown, Taneytown, Middleburg, Frederick, Jeffersonville, Crainton's Gap, Fairplay, Sharpsburg, Md., Harpers Ferry, Snickers Gap, Ashby's Gap, Manassas Gap, White Plains, Thoroughfare Gap, Greenwich, Calletts Station, Kelly's Ford to Kemper's Ford, Rappahannock River, Va. arriving there July 31st having marched about 225 miles. Since that time we have been guarding the Ford and doing picket duty along the Rapahannock River.

On the 18th of July, Andrew Gale started out from Washington to rejoin his regiment but before he could do that, he had to locate where they were. According to the entries in his diary, he was alone at first, but he did catch up with some familiar units, after about two days, and travelled with them, the 11th Corps, until the 27th of July, when at noon, he located the 137th Regiment, and "the boys", as he called them.

Saturday, July 18, 1863

Started from Washington about nine o'clock. Put up at Foolsville at night.

Sunday, July 19, 1863

Started from Foolsville about 8 o'clock, put up at noon at Point of Rocks, put up near Waterford all night.

Monday, July 20, 1863

Pleasant. Overtook the 11 Corps in the forenoon. Halted with them near Goose Creek & stayed all night. Slept very poorly for fear of something being stolen.

Tuesday, July 21, 1863

Pleasant. Stayed near Goose Creek all day. Quite uneasy. The 73rd Regt. Started on a march at almost sundown.

Wednesday, July 22, 1863

Stayed near Goose Creek all day. Pleasant & warm. Rather uneasy.

Thursday, July 23, 1863

Pleasant & warm. Started from Goose Creek. Took dinner at White Plaines. Got near Baltimore just about dark.

Friday, July 24, 1863

Pleasant & warm. Went down & see Provost Martial. Changed camp.

Saturday, July 25, 1863

Pleasant. Marched at about five o'clock. Went to Warrington Junction, stayed all night. Rained pretty hard in the night.

Sunday, July 26, 1863

Pleasant & warm. Stayed at the Junction. Write a letter to uncle   Ezra & went in swimming.

Andrew was always thinking about the family back home and wrote to them whenever he had the chance and the time. When he found his Regiment and Company K., he passed the news back to his parents and by the tone of his letter, he seemed quite pleased to be with the men again.

Warrington Junction

July 27/63

Dear Parents

I now take my opportunity to send you a few lines to inform you of my where abouts. I have found my regiment. I have been over a week getting from Washington & I got here before the Major. It seems some like old times again. The boys are all well & tough. I am well also. Uncle Ezra is tough, at least he looks so. I will not write much this time. I have permission from the Captain to take care of the Major's horse until he comes. No more this time. Tell all inquiring friends to write.

From Andrew

Monday, July 27, 1863

Pleasant & warm. Found the regiment about noon. John came over with me found the boys all well.

Tuesday, July 28, 1863

Stayed near Warrington Junction.

Wednesday, July 29, 1863

Cloudy. Went down & washed my shirt & stockings, went in swimming.

Thursday, July 30, 1863

Pleasant & warm. Stayed in camp.

July 30th/63
Near Warrington Junction

Dear Parents

I received your welcomed

letter last night & was glad to hear from you. It come rather unexpected to me, it come very near getting here before I did. I had only been here two days when I got it. I have written one letter before this since I have been to the regiment. I have been quite a while coming. I stayed at Washington four days. I started for the regiment a week ago last Saturday & was over a week getting to the regiment. I was with the 11 Corps a week. I lived with John while I stayed there. I felt rather streaked. I started on Saturday & the Major   said he would start the first of the week & I though he would get to the regiment first but I have not seen him yet. I have taken care of his horse since I have been to the regiment. I have sent in for some clothes. I expect to be dressed in blue before long. The boys are all well & enjoying themselves as well as could be expected. The weather is quite changeable. It rains a little most every day. It is rather a poor place for an army to encamp. The watter is very poor. The Army is recruiting I should think by the move of things. I suppose the drafted men will be coming here before long. They have sent me to guard them down here so they will come safe. Tell Harve they will fetch him down safe if he don't pay his three hundred.[30] Tell Daniel he had better pay his three hundred for if he should come down here he would miss his milk & maybe a bullit would make him grunt a little. I think he had better stay at home & take care of the baby. Tell the folks that want to hear from me they must write to me first. The cars run close by where we are encamped. It seems like civilization. Yesterday they were carrying pontoons on the cars towards Warrington. Some think we will cross the Rapahannock soon. There was just now a load of soldiers gone by on the cars. I can't think of any more to write this time so

---

[30] It was possible to avoid the Draft by paying $300.

.

good bye for the present Write soon & oblige your son

Andrew H. Gale

P.S. I should like to have you send me the Driden News that I had that Sunday & some writing paper. The boys were out & I have only a few sheets left. Give my love to all me & some women. Send me a pencil point.

Friday, July 31, 1863

Called early in the morning to march. Went near the Rapahannock & encamped.

The Regimental Clerk's records for the remaining days of July contained the following information

July 19th. Marched to near Hillsborough, Va.

July 20th. Marched to Snickes Gap, Va.

July 21st & 22nd. At Snickes Gap, Va.

July 23rd. Marched to Manassas Gap, Va.

July 24th. Marched to Piedmont, Va.

July 25th. Marched to Georgetown, Va.

July 26th. Marched to Carlette Station, Va.

July 27, 28, 29, 30. Lay at Carlette Station, Va. awaiting orders.

July 31st. Marched to Kempers Ford, Va. where we are now.

Aug. 1863. This command has lain at Kempers Ford, Va. guarding the ford and doing picket duty.

The month of August found Andrew Gale settled in with his regiment and getting used to Army life again. August found them with some inactivity from battle, with time to rest, and the pleasant duty of caring for the Major's horse, until the Major returned to the Regiment.

From the diary accounts and the letters written home, it was evident that part of their food supply was gathered from the land. Foraging was both an assigned duty and a personal activity, when special items were desired.

This lull in duties also allowed time for card playing, with Eucre being the game of choice, most of the time.

Saturday, August, 1, 1863
Pleasant but very warm. (Unable to read entry about cook and horsemen)

Sunday, August 2, 1863
Pleasant & warm. Stayed in camp near Kempers Ford. Went a blackberry very thick picking. Don't feel very well.

Monday, August, 3, 1863
Pleasant but very hot. Not very well

Tuesday, August 4, 1863
Pleasant & warm. Monot after days washed my shirt, got all the huckleberry I wanted to eat.

Wednesday, August 5, 1863
Pleasant & warm. Not very well. Stayed in camp most of the time. Played eucre with Ezra, John & Daton.

Thursday, August 6, 1863
Pleasant. The most of our Company are on picket. Let the Major's horse go out.

Friday, August 7, 1863
(No Entry)

Saturday, August 8, 1863
(No Entry)

(No Entry)

August 9th /63
Near Kempers Ford

Dear Parents

I received sometime last week & I can't tell when shortly after I sent one home so I thought it best to wait until Sunday for I consider it the day for me to write home. I am well & enjoying myself as well as I can & the boys are well too. I hope that these few lines will find you well also. We are encamped in a very nice place. It is very warm here now. There is considerable fruit around here. I went out today and got some huckleberries & black berries, also some green corn, good size too. I understand that the school marm thinks that I am mad at her but I guess there must be a mistake in print somewhere. I got a letter from Harve the other day. He said he was among the drafted. He thought he should pay his three hundred dollars if they would clear him for three years but I guess he will anyway, at least I hope he will. I am taking care of the Major's horse yet & expect to until he comes to the regiment. I have not heard anything from him since I left Washington. I have it very easy now. I hope we won't march from this place very soon. We have good water here. That is a thing we don't have at all places. Sometimes we have to drink muddy water but now we got about as good water as our old spring up north. It is almost night & I must bring my letter to a close. The bugle has blown for the night so good by for the present. Please write soon and oblige your son.

Andrew, give my love to all

Monday, August 10, 1863
(No Entry)

Tuesday, August 11, 1863

(No Entry)

Wednesday, August 12, 1863

Pleasant & warm. On fatigue all day.

Thursday, August 13, 1863

Stormy, Got very good quarters, can keep dry if I stay in my tent

Friday, August 14, 1863

(No Entry)

Saturday, August 15, 1863

(No Entry)

Sunday, August 16, 1863

Pleasant. Went out after some corn. Rained in the evening. Heard a very hard clap of thunder.

Monday, August 17, 1863

(No Entry)

Tuesday, August 18, 1863

(No Entry)

Wednesday, August 19, 1863

(No Entry)

Thursday, August 20, 1863

Drew five days rations for our horses. Pleasant & warm. Let the Major's horse go to Brigade Headquarters for the Captain.

Friday, August 21, 1863

Pleasant & warm. Nothing new & nothing much to do. Wrote a letter home.

Aug. 21st /63

Kempers Ford

Dear Parents

I received your letter bearing dateAug. 13th & you bet I was glad to hear from you & to hear that you are well. Your letter found me kicking around some. I am well and hope that these few lines will find you all well. We have been here in camp now nearly three weeks. I am enjoying myself as well as I did at home. I take care of the Majors horse now & have since I come to the regiment. I mess with four others besides myself & live pretty well for a soldier. I am perfectly satisfied with my place at present. I hope I never shall have to march in the ranks of the old 137 Regt again but I may you know afterall. Ezra took the watch & in your next letter I want you to let me know wheather you have paid uncle Steve the rest & if not wheather you are going to or not. Uncle Ezra wants to know how the money is a going that we sent him when he was sick. Write about all the affairs around home. Tell Harve that I wrote him a letter before I got his & have been waiting to receive an answer from that before I write again. Tell the school marm that I send my respects to her also all the girls in our neighborhood. Our camp is about a mile from the river. Our pickets & the rebel pickets are near enough to talk to each other if it was not for the river. There is a dam near our pickets and the water makes such a noise they can't hear. They seem to be very friendly to each other. The paymaster has paid off our regiment but did not pay me. He said I would have to wait until next time. I send my love to Mother, Father, Gusta, & Scott. Tell Scott & Gusta to be good children for my sake. No more at present. Please write soon and oblige your son & soldier boy.

   Andrew H. Gale

 P.S. It is very fine weather here now, cool nights & warm days. Soldiering is easy business when in camp. Don't worry about me.

    Saturday, August 22, 1863

 (No Entry)

         August 22nd /63

Dear Father

 When I wrote my letter yesterday I forgot to send for a shirt. I want you to send one of my check shirts by mail. I received the stamps you sent me & the writing paper. It is a very fine morning. There has not been very much rain since I have been here. I have seen some hot weather you bet. My citizens clothes don't come bad now. I ware them most of the time. No more this time. I am well & so are the boys. No more this time.   From Andrew

    Sunday, August 23, 1863

 Pleasant & warm. Wrote a letter home to aunt Mary

    Monday, August 24, 1863

 Pleasant & warm. Got a canteen of wiskey for forty cents.

    Tuesday, August 25, 1863

 Pleasant & cool. Showers the day, rained quite hard towards night. Drew five days ration of grain for my horse.

Ezra Bostwick, brother to Andrew's mother Chloe Gale, had designated his Brother in Law, Peter Gale, Andrews's father, to handle some business for him at home. He wrote the following letters, one to Peter with instructions regarding a business tranasaction. The other two were to his sister and his niece. Again, the letter composition and spelling show a definite absence of a formal education on Ezra's part.

Verginia   Aug. 25th 63
Camp nigh kempers fors

Dear Nece

I received your welcom letter date the 9th and I was very glad to here from you and to here that you was well. Your cind letter found me well and I hope this will find you the same. You said you hadent sen Loverna in som tim. I think you mint go and se her often. You said you and flora was going down to se her. I hope you will. Don't forget to go and se her tell her I am well and will writ son. You said there hadben a good meney blackberries and huckleberries ther this year. There has ben the most her I ever se in all my lief. There is a good meney peaches and apels and corn here so we live very well. It geten lat and I most clos my letter. writ son. this is from your uncle Ezra.

To Augusta, good by

Wednesday, August 26, 1863
(No Entry)

Aug. 26th /63

Dear Brother: I received your letter that sent to Andrew for me and was glad here from you and to here that you was well. You writ in your letter that you cod sel (could sell) the poney and I thought best to sel him if you cod. I expect he bothered you som. Writ as son as you can. I will writ more the next time.   Ezra

Verginia   Aug. 26th /63

Dear Brother Peter

I have got a little tim to

writ you a few lines to let you know that I am well and hope this few lins will find you the same. We ar left here to gard the ford. It tak quite a strong jucit to gard a long here, the rebs aron wone sid and we ar on the other. We talk together mos every day. Down the river a few mils tha toll our bois tha was gard som hay fore us. I expect tha thought General Gerry[31] dar not com over so he thought he wood save them garding it inay (any) longer so he went over Sunday and got 20 or 30 tons of hay and som cattle. How meney I do not know. Wen he crost over the ron for life. (When he crossed over they run for their life) The never fird a gun. It geten lat and I clos. Writ as son as can. Don foreget to writ. This is from your Brother.

Ezra to Peter

Aug. 26th /63

Dear Sister Chloe   I tak my pen to writ you a few lins to let you know that I hadent fore got you. You said you mist me at home but what do you think of me of (off) in this disent land all a lone without friends. I hope the tim will son com thyat I may be there ans se you all wonce more Chloe. Last night I was out on picit. It com my tim to go on at 2 oclock at night. My post was wone of the meness post I ever was on. I had to go of quite far from the rest all a lone down through a guley all bushes and there stand 2 ours (hours). My nighest friend was the foe. As I stood there wack the enema I thought of you and the rest of my friends. I began to be all most hom sick but my relief com to relive me and I went back and lay down on the ground and though know more a bough my friends till morning. Chloe, I wood lik to se you but that can't be at present. I think of you

---

[31]Brig. Gen. John White Geary, USA

87

every day. I wood lik to be there and help you eat one of your good johney cakes. I wood lik to be there a litle while and tell you what I amsen on my hard marches. Tha is so meney thing I want to tell you but I wlll quit. So writ son don't fore get to writ this is from your brother Ezra Bostwick to my sister Chloe Gale   good by

Andrew is well and enjoy himself very well. He has got quite a easy fitas (fatigue). All he does is to tak care of Majors horse. I wood lik to here from my friends often.

Dear Parents

As Ezra has written & offered me an opportunity to put in a few lines. I thought I would accept the opportunity. It is a fine day & I have slept away the biggest part of it. I got up at one o'clock. The box come very exceptable just now. If it had not been so long in coming through I should like to have another one but boxes generally come through in less than a month when they are directed right. I should like some dried apples. We don't draw any of those here. If you should make up your mind to send a small box, Ezra wants you to send him a streaked or checkered shire, one socks for himself & if Ma & Grandma want to send some socks down here to sell, we can get $1.00 a pair. If they do send them do send them do them up in separate bunches & put their name on them. If you send any cookies bake them hard. The soft ones tainted a little. A little tobacco would come good. Keep track of your expenses for me. I will try & send some money home next payday. Direct the box, if you send, as you would a letter. I don't think of anything much more to write today. My health & Ezra's are good. Give my love to all. No more this time. I ever remain your son & soldier boy.

A. H. Gale

to
P. B. Gale
&
C. M. Gale
I send a fifty cent piece

August 31.st/03
Kempers Ford

Dear Parents
I received
your letter baring date Aug
19th. I you let I was glad to
hear from you & to hear that
you are well your letter found
me kicking around some
I am well & hope that these
few lines will find you all well
we have been here in camp
now nearly three weeks I am
enjoying myself as well as
I did at home, I take care
of the Majors horse now I
have since I come to the
regiment I mess with four
others beside myself & live
pretty well for a soldier I
am perfectly satisfied with

Thursday, August 27, 1863

(No Entry)

Friday, August 28, 1863

Pleasant & warm. Went down to the ford and got uncle Ezra's gun to clean for inspection. Played eucre some. Come up to camp got a sheet of emory paper off N Williams.

Saturday, August 29, 1863

Pleasant & warm. Was to have inspection but did not have it. It rained some in the afternoon.

Sunday, August 30, 1863

Pleasant but cool. Drew five days ration of grain for the horses. Went down towards the river to find my horse.

Monday, August 31, 1863

Pleasant & warm. Layed around. We had inspection & muster.

Chapter Six

The month of September began as August had ended, with no action to speak of and the soldiers doing regular military duties such as guard duty, picket duty, and Provost duties.

The normal time for letter writing was available and Andrew took advantage of it to keep his family, at home, informed as to his life in the army. They continued to forage for food, for themselves, and for their animals.

The regiment remained at Kempers Ford, Va.., until September 15th. On that date they received orders to march and proceeded to Kelly's Ford.

Before returning to Andrew Gale's diary and letters, it is important to know that a change in the Army's structure was about to take place.

To this point in time, the 137th Regiment, N.Y.S.V., was part of the 12th Army Corps, Army of the Potomac, and it spent 1862 and the first eight months of 1863, in the eastern sections, and battles, of the war zone.

In the latter part of September, they were transported to the western sector of the war and in October, 1863, they were attached to the 3rd Brigade, 2nd Division, 20th Corps, Army of the Cumberland.

The first record of the transfer is from the Regimental Clerks Report:

Sept. 1863. No statement. Report dated Bellaire, Ohio. Oct, 20

Field & Staff Muster Roll:

Sept. & Oct 1863 Lookout Valley, Tenn. Nov. 16, 63
The regiment remained at Kempers Ford, Va. until Sept. 18

when we left at 6 P.M., marched to Bealton, the Rapidan, crossed the Rappahannock at Kelly's Ford, went into camp at Racoon Ford and remained there until Sept. 24 when we started for Washington, D.C. Load the Reg't on cars at Bealton Station, Va. on the 28th, arrived at Washington in the evening of the same day. Immediately proceeding to the Relay House thence via B & O R.R., to the Ohio River arriving at Bellaire, O. 4 miles below Wheeling, Va. thence via Ohio Central R.R. To Indianapolis, Ind. South to Louisville, Ky. Thence to Nashville, Tenn. Remained at Nashville 6 days being detached from the Brig. to escort the 11th Corps wagon train on its way to Chattanooga as far as Dischord, T. Via marching and guarding said train to Dischord passing Murfreesboro, Shelbyville, Tullahoma & returned to Fosterville, T. Remained 3 days and embarked again by rail for Bridgeport, Ala. Passing Stevenson, Ala.
Oct. 27. Left Bridgeport at 2 P.M. Arrived at Shelmound & bivouacked with the Brigade for the night. Morning of the 28th took up our line of march for Lookout Mtn. Arrived at the base of it at sunset & encamped for the night. About 12 o'clock was called suddenly into line of battle on the extreme left and a terrific battle ensued lasting 2 1/2 hours. Heavy firing on our pickets betakening an attack from the enemy, soon marched out of the woods, took position in line of battle on the left. Our Reg't behaved nobly, standing the whole brunt of the battle & remaining at the close (when enemy retreated) in the exact position which it had taken at the onset. Our loss showed plainly which Reg't did the fighting as all of the other Reg"ts lost but a trifling number. Our loss was 15 killed and 75 woulded including Lt. Col. Van Vorhees in left side. Buried the dead on the 29th. Rested the 30th and left the Battlefied Wauhatchie the 31st directly after mustering.

The Company K, bi monthly report reads:

Sept. & Oct. 1863 Wauchatchie, Tenn

On the 15th. Sept. 1863, we broke camp at Kempers Ford and marched via Kelly's Ford to Raccoon Ford at which place we arrived on the day following. Here we remained until Sept. 29th when we again received marching orders and moved to Bealton Station where we took the cars for Washington, D.C. Thence by rail to Relay House, thence by B & O R.R. To Bentwood where we crossed the Ohio to Bellaire from whence we were transported on the Ohio Central R.R. To Indianapolis, Ind. Thence by rail to Nashville, Tenn. Via Jeffersonville and Louisville. Here we were tempororily detached from the Brigade to escort the 11th Corps wagon train on its way to Chattanooga. We marched with the train as far as Discord passing through Murfreesboro, Shelbyville, Tohuloma Then retraced our steps to Fosterville, Tenn where we remained until the 26th when agreeable to orders we took the cars to Bridgeport at which place we arrived Oct. 27th. We then moved via Shellmound to Lookout Mountain reaching said mountain at sunset on the 28th where we bivouacked for the night. At midnight we were suddenly arroused by the approach of the enemy when we quietly formed in line and fought a mostly superior force for about three hours. After which the enemy retired leaving his dead & wounded in our works. The fight was a desperate one and the men fought bravely. Comp. K, lost 4 killed & 8 wounded.

Andrew Gale's account of this period, from September 1, 1863 to the end of October, recorded in his diaries and letters, gives light to just how the men in the ranks spent their time. The diary relates the types of duties performed, by the enlisted men and the letters contain news of battles and movements that were important to the parents and friends at home in New York state.

The first part of September was rather uneventful, with no

action to speak of and very little movement.

Tuesday, September 1, 1863

Pleasant. Not very well. Wrote a letter home. J Flemming received two letters from Groton.

Wednesday, September 2, 1863

Pleasant & warm. On camp guard. Sick all night.

Thursday, September 3, 1863

Pleasant. Relieved about ten oclock. Not very well all day.

Friday, September 4, 1863

Pleasant & warm. Feel quite well. This morning drew 5 days rations of grain for the horse.

Saturday, September 5, 1863

Detailed on guard. Pleasant & warm.

Sunday, September 6, 1863

Pleasant & warm. Wrote 2 letters. One home & one to Harve. Not very well.

Sept. 6th /63
Kempers Ford, Va.

Dear Father

I received your welcomed letter night before last & was glad to hear from home. I assure you it found me well & I hope this epistle will find you & the rest of the family also. I am glad to think that blackberries are as plenty as they are. They were very thick here some time ago but they are all gone long ago. We have grapes now & peaches are almost ripe. So near they begin to taste quite peach fashion. Corn is getting almost to hard to eat. We had some for dinner. Some of it was so hard we could hardly eat it. I suppose its some forwarder than it is in old Groton. If Daniel had come down here I think we could of furnished him with milk for we have it most every day regular. (Mr Webb must not worry to much about me for when they catch me they will have to play smart). I hope he will have good luck. I hope he won't get drowned while to work at his hay & you say that Burr has got his back up. You can tell him to kiss my ankle for I ask no odds of him & if he wants anything of me he must wait until I come home or he comes down here a conscript. If he thinks I coaxed off Romain (Romain is a male) why on earth didn't he speak to me when I was at home when I could play my part. Confound a sneak. Tell Frank to be a good boy. My advise would be for him to stay away from Burrs if he knows himself but he can do as he is a mind to for all of me. I should like to of been to Meads funeral although I should of felt sorrowful. If I ever get home, I shall miss Mead very much. I expect I shall get all of my pay next payday although I may get sucked in though but I guess not. The boys think that I will get it. I have been mustered in for my pay quite a spell. I have talked with Ezra & he said that if you have sold the colt, he would like to have you mention it in your next. He thinks you had not better pay John Sharpstein any more if he got the oats for he thought that the oats would nearly pay him if not more. He said he thought he had paid you for the oats he had borrowed. If not he wants you to let him know. He thought that when he settled with you he turned on the buggy but he wanted you to let him know how it stood. Probably he will come home this winter if we go into camp this winter & I hope we will for it is not very pleasant to be marching around all winter. We are in a nice place to go into winter quatters. There is a cleard lot in the woods of about 10 or 12 acres. We are on the south side of the lot just in the edge of the woods & the 111th Pa. Regiment is on the north side of the lot just on the edge of the woods. The nicest place we were ever encamped on. I liked to forget to state why I did not get my pay. The reason was that I was not mustered in. I think there will be no trouble next time. You need not send that shirt if it costs so much. I had heard Greenfield but nothing about Rowly & hide. I think Sharp has got to a nice place now. Give my love to all. There is not room to mention all the names. No more this time. Write soon & oblige your son.

A. H. Gale

Monday, September 7, 1863

Pleasant & warm. Detailed on picket but put on camp guard for a spell while Dave Nolle went up to the Brigade. Moved my house. Took til dark.

Tuesday, September 8, 1863

Pleasant & warm. Detailed on guard, was number one before guard house

Wednesday, September 9, 1863

(No Entry)

Thursday, September 10, 1863

(No Entry)

Friday, September 11, 1863

(No Entry)

Saturday, September 12, 1863

Pleasant & warm. Detailed on guard. Expected inspection. Rained in the night.

Sunday, September 13, 1863

Pleasant & warm. Wrote a letter home. Went up to the Brigade & got the mail. Did not eat any supper.

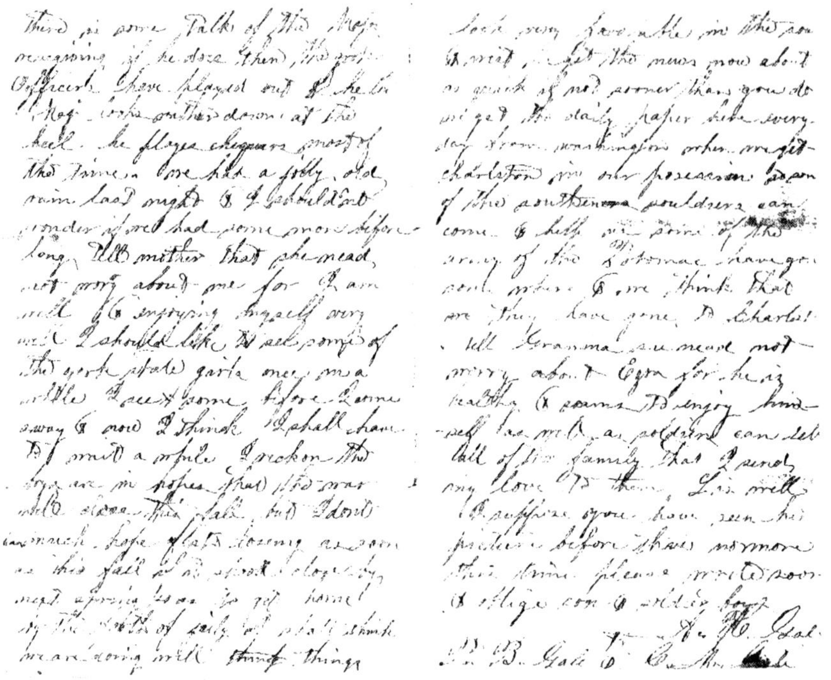
there is some talk of the Major
resigning if he does then, the [illegible]
Officers have played out & he [illegible]
Maj [illegible] another down at the
heel. he plays checkers most of
the time & [illegible] like a jolly. had
rain last night & I shouldn't
wonder if we had some more before
long, tell mother that she need
not worry about me for I am
well & enjoying myself very
well I should like to see some of
the york state girls once more a
little I see some before I come
away & now I think I shall have
to wait a while I reckon the
boys are in hopes that the war
will close this fall, but I don't
much hope of its closing as soon
as this fall [illegible]
next spring [illegible] to get home
[illegible]
we are doing well [illegible] things

look very favorable in the [illegible]
[illegible] get the news now about
as quick if not sooner than you do
we get the daily paper here every
day from washington when we get
Charleston in our possession soon
of the southern soldiers can
come & help [illegible] of the
army of the Potomac have gone
south where [illegible] think that
[illegible] they have gone to Charleston
tell Granma she need not
worry about Ezra for he is
healthy & seems to enjoy himself as well as soldiers can tell
all of the family that I send
my love to them, Liz well
I suppose you have seen his
picture before this no more
this time please write soon
& oblige your [illegible] boy
[illegible] H. Gale
[illegible] B. Gale [illegible]

Sept 13th.,/63

Kempers Ford, Va.

Dear Parents

I take this opportunity to inform you how I get along. I am well and hope these few lines will find you enjoying the same blessing. I have answered your last letter but it being my custom to write every Sunday, I thought I send you a few lines. We have been laying still quite a spell but expect to march everyday. Orders come today to be ready to march at any moment. There has been canonading on our right all day. We have got things so comfortable I hate to leave here it is so pleasant too, watter handy & very good. There is some talk of the Major resigning. If he does then the Groton Officers have played out. He, the "Maj" looks rather down at the heel. He playes chequars most of the time. We had a jolly old rain last night & I shouldn't wonder if we had some more before long. Tell mother that she need not worry about me for I am well & enjoying myself very well. I should like to see some of the York state girls once in a while. I see some before I come away & now I think I shall have to wait a while. I reckon the boys are in hopes that the war will close this fall but I don't have much hope of its closing as soon as this fall. If it should close by next spring so as to get home by the fourth of July, I shall think we are doing well. Things look very favorable in the south & west. We get the news now about as quick if not sooner than you do. We get the daily papers here every day. From Washington. When we get Charleston in our possession so some of the southern soldiers can come & help us. Some of the Army of the Potomac have gone somewhere and we think that they have gone to Charleston. Tell Grandma she need not worry about Ezra for he is healthy & seems to enjoy himself as well as a soldier can. Tell all of the family that I send my love to them. L is well. I suppose you have seen his picture before this. No more this time. Please write soon & oblige son & soldier boy.

A. H. Gale
P. B. Gale & C. M. Gale

Monday, September 14, 1863

Pleasant & warm. Went out after milk. Got two canteens of milk from Mrs Kempers cows. Went around to the ford., drove up the mules and horses.

Tuesday, September 15, 1863
Pleasant & warm. Went out with the boys and got some
corn with the horses, got a bag full & got dinner. Fell very
well. Sent my letter down to Ezra, got order to march, went to
Kelly's Ford.

In the Regimental report records, the shift of the 137th
Regiment from Virginia and the Army of the Potomac, to the West,
and the Army of the Cumberland, began taking place on this date.
Andrew tells how it effected he and the rest of the "boys"
The troops were transported, for the most part, on top of
freight cars. This was not the most comfortable means of travel, but it
was much better than marching the thousands of miles to the western
front, and that was the only other means of transportation.

Wednesday, September 16, 1863
Cloudy. Started before daylight and crossed the river then
halted a spell. Then crossed the Rappahannock, got to
Fredericksburg about two oclock, went out on picket, went on
picket twice. Not very well.

Thursday, September 17, 1863
Foggy. Orders to march at seven. Marched oart of the day,
stopped quite a spell about noon, stopped for the night. Not
very well. Through the day the Paymaster come to the
Regiment just before night.

Friday, September 18, 1863
Stormy & quite cool. I guess Paymaster payed off the
Regiment. Two men shot today. I saw a corpse, a bad looking
sight. Bought a locket.

Saturday, September 19, 1863
Cold & cloudy. Had inspection by Capt Shipman. Wrote

home & sent my check of $110. Went out with the boys after hay & uncle Ezra wrote to Lilas son. Bought some letters a star also some figures.

Sunday, September 20, 1863
Pleasant & warm. Went out after hay couldn't get any. Then went out another way & got some sweet potatoes. Stayed in my tent the rest of the day & read a book.

Monday, September 21, 1863
Pleasant & warm. Detailed on picket. Major started for home this morning He gave me his blankets & over coat. Very cold at night. Stood tours in the night. Come in after the ration.

Tuesday, September 22, 1863
Pleasant & warm. Come off picket about eleven o clock, drew 8 days rations. Wrote two letters & one more. Slept with John Foot, Marve Williams got his picture taken.

Wednesday, September 23, 1863
Pleasant & warm. Drilled on company drill after dinner. Had Battalion drill & dress parade. Got up rather late.

Thursday, September 24, 1863
Pleasant & warm. Started on a tramp. Stoped for the night. Slept very well, stayed in a nice place.

Friday, September 25, 1863
Pleasant & warm. Marched a small distance & encamped for the day & night.

Saturday, September 26, 1863
Pleasant & cool. Got up before daylight with orders to march. Went to Brandy Station from there to Rappahannock

from there to Bralaton Station. I was detailed on guard.

Sunday, September 27, 1863
Pleasant & warm. Stayed around all day. Read a magazine though had the headache all the afternoon & night. Did not sleep any all night.

Monday, September 28, 1863
Pleasant & warm. Felt quite well. Start for the cars, halted for the cars to get ready until almost one. Got to Washington after dark, stayed there two or three hours. Got some refreshments.

Tuesday, September 29, 1863
Pleasant & warm. Got to Harpers Ferry about noon. Rode on top of the cars most all of the way. Got to Martinburg sun about an hour high. Rode all night. Got to Freemont about three o'clock.

Wednesday, September 30, 1863
Pleasant & warm. Started from W. Va about six o'clock got to Grafton sun an hour high got to Fairmont about sundown got to farmington after dark. Rode all night on the cars. Arrived in Bentwood about daylight.

For a young farm boy from rural New York state, what was happening was quite an adventure. This was possibly the first time that Andrew Gale was this far away from his natural enviorenment. The tone and the contents of his letters to the family are not those of a soldier on his way to do battle with the enemy, but those of a young man, seeing a new part of his country for the first time. Thoughts of army events did occupy some of his thinking, but for the most part, he wanted to tell the folks at home, what he was seeing enroute, for the first time.

Cranberry Summit   Sept. 30th /63

Dear Parents   I suppose you
will be somewhat surprised to hear from me here. I am over
100 miles west & north of Harpers Ferry on the Baltimore &
Ohio R. R. I suppose I shall be in Ohio long before you get
this. I think we are going to Tennessee. The 11 Corps & the
12th Corps are goin the same way. The 11th has gone ahead. I
am well & so are the boys. I sent you a letter over a week ago
& received no answer. I sent a check of $110.00. I should like
to hear from it before long. When you send me a little money.
Traveling on the cars takes a lot of cash. I have not much to
write this time. The cars will start before long. I suppose when
we get to our stopping point I will write again. I hope this will
find you well. No more this time, give my love to all. Today
is verry warm. Please write soon. Direct as before until you
hear from me again. From your son & soldier.

A. H. Gale

Thursday, October 1, 1863

Pleasant & warm. Find myself on the banks of the Ohio
river waiting for the cars. Crossed the river about daylight to a
village called Bellair. Stayed all day & night. Rained all night or
nearly.

Friday, October 2, 1863

Pleasant & warm. Started on the cars about 11 oclock, got
to Zanesville a little before sundown, got to Columbus about
nine oclock. Slept very nice all night on the cars.

Saturday, October 3, 1863

Pleasant & warm. Got to West Dayton in the morning a little after sunrise. Arrived at Richmond[32] about 12 oclock, started away about 4. Run over to Centerville. They gave us something to eat.

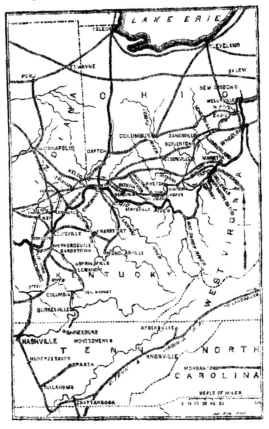

---

[32]Richmond, Indiana, located in eastern Indiana near the Ohio border

Richmond, Ind. Oct 3, /63

Dear Parents

I thought I would inform you I am well, We have been in Ohio two days. One day we layed on the banks of the Ohio River & one day & night on the cars. We have just got in the edge of Ind. In a small place called Richmond. We are on the cars waiting for the cars to go on. We have thought that we were going to Tenn. & I don't know that we will as it is. It is raining quite hard now. It has been quite fine weather & we have had a gay old ride, you bet some four or five hundred miles. The boys are well and so am I. I have seen some very nice land since I have been on the road. I think you are foolish to stay in York state & grub around the stone. Here the land is free from stone & the crops look nice indeed. A great deal of corn is raised out in these parts. I havn't received any letter since we started. I will write again soon if nothing happens supposing you would like to hear from me often. No more this time. Give my love to all. From your son.

A. H. Gale
In Richmond, Ind. Oct. 3

to
Peter B. Gale

Sunday, October 4, 1863

Cloudy & cold. Arrived at Indianapolis about one oclock a. m. Stayed until about noon. Arrived at Franklin about dark. Road all night on the cars some of the time on the engine.

Monday, October 5, 1863

Pleasant & cool. Arrived at Jeffersonville about daylight. Crossed the Ohio river into Kentucky in the city of Louisville. Started away about noon. Arrived at Elizabethtown about dark. Rode on the cars all night.

Tuesday, October 6, 1863

Pleasant & warmer than it was yesterday. Arrived at a small village called Galatin. Arrived at Nashville little before noon. Got off ot the cars & struck tents in the south part of the city. Rained all night

Wednesday, October 7, 1863

Pleasant & cool. Washed my shirt and stockings this morning. Found quite a Brigade I reckon. Stayed around camp most of the day. Four from the company went to the theater.

Thursday, October 8, 1863

Pleasant & warm. Wrote a letter home. Detailed on horse duty. Had drilled most of the day. Took a walk up to the..in the evening, did not get back until after revilee.

In the next letter, written home by Andrew Gale, he seems impressed that he is nearing Nashville, Tennessee. He describes the city as being large and he has hopes they might remain there for some time. Rumors told the men they were being picked for special duty by General Slocum and this was good news, since they were somewhat tired from their long trip from Virginia.

Nashville, Tenn Oct 8/63
Dear Parents

I now find myself in the edge of the city of Nashville Tennessee. We arrived here day before yesterday. It has been quite stormy & cold since we come here until today & now it seems quite pleasant. What we stoped here for is more than I can tell. The rest of our Corps has gone on to Chattanooga as near as I can find out & yesterday there was an officer read a line from the Colonel giving us praise for our good behavior on the road & that General Slocum had stoped us here to do some special duty on that account. Some say we are going to stay here two or three weeks & some say it is a permanent thing that we are going to do provost duty in this city. I hope it may be so although it most to good news & to nice work for the 137th to do. This is a large city. I have not been around in it much yet. Four from our Company have a pass to go up town so I think I shall have a chance to see the city before long. We had a long ride on the cars. We rode on them eight days & nights. We pass through a great many nice places but of all the states I have seen yet, Ind., goes ahead for soil. We passed through Capitol of Ohio, Ind., & Tenn. I don't know how much farther we may go but I hope we may stay here a spell yet. I have seen so much to but that I have entirely bought myself out. I want you to send me, in your next, a sheet of greenbacks with the V on it. We are here where we can buy things & it seems rather tough to be without money. I have borrowed a dollar already. I have not received any letters for about two weeks. I want you write as soon as you get this. I would like to hear from home very well & friends also. I have not much to write although I suppose you will think that I might a good long. I am on fatigue today so I must cut my letter short for we have no light to write by night. This leaves me well & the rest of the boys. Ezra has quite a cold so I will bid you goodbye. Hoping to hear from you soon. Give my love to all. Please write soon and oblige your son.

A. H. Gale
Direct your letters to
Nashville, Tennessee
instead of Washington, D. C.

Federal Outer Line. Nashville, Tenn

Oct 9

Yesterday I was to late for the mail so I had to wait until today.I find myself well still in Nashville. Talk some of leaving tomorrow. If we do I will write again soon otherwise I think I shall wait for an answer.

Friday, October 9, 1863

Pleasant & warm. Had six eggs for breakfast, some cheese, dried beef & bread. No drill. Went over to the river & took a wash. Not much to do through the day. Stoddard went to the theater in the evening.

Saturday, October 10, 1863

Pleasant & warm. Drill some in the forenoon. Ezra not very well. He got a very bad cold. Stayed around camp all day, nothing to do Played Calafornia some in the daytime & in the night.

Sunday, October 11, 1863

Pleasant but cloudy. Detailed on guard, had inspection. Had sweet potatoes for supper. Some stormy through the night.

The stay in Nashville was not as extended as the men had hoped for and on October 12, they received their orders to march. They travelled quite a long distance over the next three or four weeks. During this time, the men foraged for food for themselves, in addition to eating army food, when it was available. The menu, while not always the most nutritious, was varied, based on what could be found in the fields closeby. Foraging for food was not always the safest activity, since Rebel soldiers took great joy in catching the Federals, out away from their units.

Monday, October 12, 1863

Stormy. Had some fried bread for breakfast. Struck tents about nine oclock & stood around in the rain until about noon. It stopped raining and we started on a march, commenced raining about 3 mi from.. It rained until most morning. Arrived at Bacirne about 8. Started to guard a supply train.

Tuesday, October 13, 1863

Rather lousy. Fell in to march about 7 oclock. Rode in the wagon all day. Rained some through the day. Got to Murpheysborough just at night. Stayed all night. Found my blanket, Bostwich lost hid knapsack. Received two letters. Still with rain.

Wednesday, October 14, 1863

Cloudy this morning. Started with the train about eight oclock. Rode all day. Arrived at Shelbyville about ten oclock P. M. Got some supper, slept in a brick building. Slept very good.

Thursday, October, 15, 1863
Stormy. Rained most of the day. Stayed at Shelbyville today. Took the load out of my gun and cleaned it up. Stayed in a brick building all night. Rained all night.

Shelbyville, Tenn. Oct. 15/63

Dear Parents

I received your kind letter bearing date lastly Sept. 22 & was glad to hear from you & to hear you were well. Your letter found me well. I was at Murpheysborough when I received it. I received one also from H. Cook at the same time. It was the first mail I has received since we left Old Virginia. We are a kind of traveling machine now. We are guarding a supply train now that belongs to the Eleventh Corps. How far we are going & where I am unable to say. We have been with train with today, four days. Today we lay by for something. We started from Nashville, Monday about noon & marched about 15 miles. Since then we have rode in the wagons. We have come about 50 miles from Nashville. We have a great many reports but it looks as though we were going to guard duty somewhere. Some think that we will go back to NV & guard the 12th Corps train through our division. The most of it is guarding places through where we have come. Two or three to Murpheysborough & they say they are ordered to fix up for winter quarters. A fellow told me today that the Colonel said there would be thirty days furloughs given to the boys. Probably uncle E will come home if he gets a good chance but I think it hardly fist for me to come if I get a chance. I had spent so much money a traveling. Now it is quite stormy here about now it has rained, four days now it is raining yet. I suppose we will start in the morning but I don't care wheather it rains or shines as long as I can ride in a top wagon. It is almost dark & I must close for this time. Please excuse all mistakes & poor writing & this dirty sheet for

I have lost all my paper & portfilio & needle book.

From A. Gale

Friday, October 16, 1863

Pleasant & warm. Started with the train about eight oclock. Got the knapsack carried, walked most of the time, found a very rough road, arrived at Tullahoma after dark. Slept in the wagon. Crossed Duck River

Saturday, October 17, 1863

Pleasant & warm. Was all the forenoon getting ready for inspection. Had inspection about noon. Got orders to remain at Tullahoma until morning. Struck tents, wrote a letter. Rained some of the night.

Sunday, October 18, 1863

Stormy in the morning. Started on the train, walked about half the way then got in the wagon & rode. Arrived at Decker about four oclock, got supper. Struck tents, drew two days rations. Went to bed. Crossed Elk River

Monday, October 19, 1863

Pleasant & warm. Started on a backward march towards Tullahoma. Marched very easy through the day. Arrived at Tullahoma just before sundown. Struck tents. Slept very well through the night. Crossed Elk River.

Tuesday, October 20, 1863

Pleasant & warm. Got up before sunrise. Started in the morning. Took dinner at a station called Orman. Crossed Duck River in the afternoon. Stoped at Slocums headquarters just at night. Rained all night.

Wednesday, October 21, 1863

Stormy this morning. Marched up to Wartract station. Stayed at the station all day. It rained considerable through the day. The cars come along about dark. We got aboard & rode down to Fosterville station.

Thursday, October 22, 1863

Pleasant & warm this morning, ate rather a small breakfast, fixed up our tent, left Stoddard & went on with Jennings & Westbrook. Got a very nice house. Picked out nails & fetched shingles most of the afternoon.

Friday, October 23, 1863

Stormy & cold most of the day. Fetched brick & stone in the forenoon. In the afternoon laid a fireplace. Fritz & Josh fetched mud, I done the mason work, Uncle E fetched some stone, spent a fine evening by the fire.

Saturday, October 24, 1863

Cloudy & cold. Got some pancakes for breakfast. Lots of the boys come to our house to warm. Detailed on picket, wrote a letter home. My post was west of the railroad. Went to camp just sundown. Got my supper.

Sunday, October 25, 1863

Pleasant but cool. Went out with Potter & got some corn for supper. Relieved about eleven, wrote two letters. Rather short of rations. Got on the cars about nine. Stoped at Bellbuckle to get our pickets.

Monday, October 26, 1863

Pleasant & warm. This morning found myself in Fisher. Took breakfast & stayed there all day. Found some apples & a pie. Traveled some through the day. Started about 8 & rode all night.

Tuesday, October 27, 1863
Cloudy & cool. Found myself in Stevison this morning. Got some crackers & a pie for breakfast. Started about nine, got to Bridgeport about noon. Got off of the cars & marched acrossed the Tennessee. Encamped near the salt peter works for the night.

Wednesday, October 28, 1863
Stormy in the morning. Started about six oclock. Rather slipery traveling. Stoped and got dinner at a place called Etna, stoped about an hour. Halted for the night. Was called up about eleven o clock. Had a fight, lost twelve killed & wounded at the battle of Wauhatchie.

The deeper the Union forces traveled into enemy territory, the more resistance they encountered. Much of the time was spent in building fortifications such as breastworks and entrenchments and this had to be done every time the regiment moved to a new location.

Thursday, October 29, 1863
Pleasant & warm. Finished or stoped about daylight. Got breakfast, relieved about seven o clock. Went back in the woods, stacked our guns & visited through the day. The Rebs shelled us most all day. Called up in the fore part of the night to build grid works. Late before we are done.

Friday, October 30, 1863
Cold and rainy this morning. Foggy. I guess the Rebs can't see us. Stayed in the entrenchments all day. Rained all day. Built a tent toward night. Got some brush & put in our tent so we slept quite soft but some wet. Rained most of the night.

Saturday, October 31, 1863

Cloudy & cold. Still in the entrenchments. Mustered in about ten o clock wrote a letter home. Ordered to march. Started about noon, went up on a hill & layed there until night. The Colonel come about sundown. Built breastworks all night. Received 2 letters from Frank

November of 1863, saw the action intensify for the 137th Regiment, as they, along with the rest of the 20th Corps, fought their way deeper into the South and enemy country. Much of the time was spent in fortifying the positions occupied by the different units.Although the first three week of the month were spent digging in building breastworks, the final week of November, saw the troops again on the move.

Chapter Seven

The Regimental Clerks record had no entry but simply stated:

Nov. 63-Wauhatchie near Chattanooga, Tenn.

The Field & Staff Muster Roll contained somewhat more descriptive information:

Nov. & Dec. 1863   The 137th Reg't remained in camp on a spur of Raccoon Mts jetting out into Lookout Valley from Nov. 1, 63 until Nov. 24 digging trenches, chopping & other fatigue duties.

Nov. 25 rec'd orders to march at half past five A. M. The 24th when we crossed Lookout Valley and Creek forming lines of battle up the slope of the Mts at right angles with the creek then swept rapidly forward in conjunction with the other Regts of the Brigade driving the Rebel skirmishers upon their lines where we charged bayonets putting them to flight and dislodging them from every position.

Nov. 25th marched across Chattanooga Valley & Creek & were engaged in the fight on Missionary Ridge supporting the Batteries of Hooker's command.

Nov. 26. moved in pursuit of Bragg's[33] force. Engaging on Bea Line Creek. Continued in pursuit on Nov. 27 & found the enemy strongly posted in Taylor Ridge, south of Ringold, Ga. We were engaged at the enterance of the Gap holding the enemy in check. Remained in Ringold until Dec. 1 when we marched back to our old camp where we remained doing fatigus duty the remainder of the month.

---

[3]General Braxton Bragg, CSA

Gen. Joseph Hooker

Two opposing Generals Officers are mentioned in the above report and both of these men gained fame in earlier stages of the war. The Union General referred to, is General Joseph Hooker, known to his men as "Fighting Joe".

General Hooker was a Colonel in the State Militia at the start of th Civil War and rose to the rank of Brigadier General, USA, in September of 1862. He had many commands during his career, but at this time, he was commanding the 20th Corps, Army of the Cumberland and continued in this capacity until July 28, 1864.

The second name recorded, in the records above, was "Bragg's force", and this was the Confederate General who the Federals were combating.

Braxton Bragg was born in North Carolina and graduated from West Point in 1837. He too, held many commands, in the Confederate Army, beginning with the Army of Pensacola, in early 1861, up to the present time, when he held the rank of General and commanded the Dept. of Tenn and later, the Dept. of North Carolina. General Bragg commanded the Army of Mississippi, on four seperate occassions.

Company K's Muster Roll, for November and December, contains the following:

Nov. & Dec. 1863 Wauchatchie, Tenn   On the morning of Nov. 24, 63, we left camp and marched in an easterly direction, crossed Lookout Creek about 9 o'clock AM and commenced the ascent of Lookout Mountain. We with the rest of our Division were formed in line of battle. The right resting near the base of the perpendicular cliffs on the summit of the mountain and reaching from thence to the creek on our left. In this form we moved forward driving the enemy at every point until late in the afternoon when the roar of musketry gradually died away and the enemy fell back leaving us in possession of an important position near the peak of the mountain and on the left flank of General Bragg's Army. Here we bivouacked for the night during which time the rebels retreated to Mission Ridge. On the following day we continued the chase, assisted in dislodging the enemy from his new position. From thence we followed him to Pea Vine Creek where we had a slight skirmish with his rear guard on the night of the 26th. On the 27th we pursued the retreating foe as far as Ringold, Ga. Where we fought him a hard battle and were victorious. We remained in this place a few days after which we set fire to the town and marched back to our old camp on Raccoon Mountain. The loss of Company K during the entire campaign was three wounded

Sunday, November 1, 1863

Pleasant & warm. Uncle Ezra got breakfast before I got up.
Moved from one hill to another about noon. Built breastworks
in the afternoon. Slept with our cartridge box on, the guns
were in the rifle pits on lookout post.

Monday, November 2, 1863

Pleasant but cloudy. Relieved in the morning. Dug in the
breastworks most all day. The Col. made quite a blow because
we were not to work. Shaved in the forenoon, put up a tent in
the afternoon, got supper after dark.

Tuesday, November 3, 1863

Pleasant & warm. Made a bed in our tent & worked on the breastworks still on a hill. Got supper about four o'clock, layed around all night. Cannons to be heard towards night. Had a good bed to sleep on. Wrote two letters to Frank.

Wednesday, November 4, 1863

Pleasant & warm. Detailed on picket. Had some beef for breakfast, detailed on picket. Stayed in camp until almost noon. Drew rations for two days. They are to last three days. A large fire on Lookout Mountain in the evening.

Thursday, November 5, 1863

Stormy in the morning. Stood on post from five til seven rained quite hard. Relieved from picket about ten o'clock. Rained all day and night. Fixed up our tent & mended my coat & stockings. Got two letters & some writing paper & needle case.

Tenn. Nov. 5th/63

Dear Parents

I received your welcome letter bearing date Oct. 25 today & one from Elmina also some writing paper, envelopes, & a needle book with some small change in it. I have some of the money left you sent me a while ago. There is not much of a chance to spend money where we are now. We are stationed on a hill some like Boliver Heights but there are more breastworks here than there was there. The needle book come just in time. My stocking needed mending. I had used most all of uncle A thread so we should have been out of that soon. Everything that is in it, I guess will come in play. I want you to send me a few things in news papers. Some have tobacco sent to them in that way. You can do up nearly a quarter of a pound & it will not cost any more.

If you can do up, uncle A's razor & send it you may hone it up good & sharp before you send it. Uncle A says tell Grandma she may send him a pair of storkings by mail. If you can't get them in one paper you can send one sock in a paper. The papers will come handy to use in doing up our meat. I should like to see the Dryden News once in a while & they are rather scarce. I want you to send me some of the small kind of pencil points. I have got a silver pencil & the points you sent don't fit the pencil. They do the brass one though. I have a gold pen but no ink. It has been quite pleasant weather here but today it is rather stormy. I went on picket yesterday & come in today. Yesterday was warm as a fellow could wish for. It is quite warm for the time of year. I forgot to speak of Stoddard on my other letter. He had a piece of his nose shot off. Quite a number of our boys got bullets put through their knapsacks & haversacks but if the bullet did not come any nearer a fellow than that it wouldent seem so hard. Some of the boys have very short notice. It is almost night & I must close. This leaves me well. Uncle A is rather under the weather now. He has had the diaria & that makes a fellow feel kind of mean. I don't suppose it would be of much use for to send me a box for I shouldend ever expect to see it. No more this time.

from your son & soldier boy

A. H. Gale

P.S. I received your postage stamps, eight in number.

Friday, November 6, 1863

Pleasant & warm. Was most ot the forenoon cleaning my gun. Uncle E marked off duty today. Mended my socks in the afternoon. Wrote a letter to uncle Harris, got supper about dark, had some popcorn in the evening.

Saturday, November 7, 1863

Pleasant & warm. Detailed on picket. Drew three quarters

rations of hardtack this morning, detailed on picket, got out on post about eleven. Wrote a letter to uncle Nathan. Stood post three times during the night. It was a very cold night.

Sunday, November 8, 1863
Pleasant & warm. The boys come with some fresh beef just as I got my breakfast ready. The rebels keep their old story with their cannon today. Wrote a letter to Elmina. Had three meals of fried beef. It was quite cold through the night. Slept quite good.

Monday, November 9, 1863
Pleasant but cool. Stood from seven until nine. Went into camp & got my breakfast. Got back on picket about two o'clock. Went on at three. Took off post in about an hour. The pioneers are chopping in front. Boiled some corn for supper.

Tuesday, November 10, 1863
Pleasant & cold. Stood on post about an hour in the morning. Got some milk and hotcakes for uncle Ezra. Went in camp and got breakfast. Relieved from picket about eleven o'clock. Fetched in some hog. Uncle Ezra seems to have a better appatite.

Wednesday, November 11, 1863
Pleasant & cool. Had some hog & beef for breakfast. Detailed on guard. Went on post at eleven o'clock, stood two hours then went over to the regiment & got my dinner. Very easy guard duty. On only four hours out of 24. Slept in a hurry. Got up ate a lot of popcorn.

Thursday, November 12, 1863
Pleasant & warm. Did not get back from breakfast until the guard was relieved. Helped Davient down a tree to fix our tent,

fooled around all day. Got an order from Fritz King for some flour, sugar 2 lbs, flour 2 pounds.

Friday, November 13, 1863
Pleasant & warm. Detailed on fatigue. Got up before daylight, got my breakfast, had some pancakes & flour gravy. Started to work at half past six o'clock. Went about five miles. Took it cool most of the day. Got to camp about dark.

Saturday, November 14, 1863
Stormy in the morning. Detailed work on the road. Got breakfast before daylight. Started to work in the rain. Stoped before we got to our destination. Worked on the road to the landing. Quit work so we got to camp before dark. Supper was ready.

Sunday, November 15, 1863
Pleasant & warm. Detailed on guard to headquarters. Had some coffee and hardtack for breakfast. Inspection this morning as usual. Come on the 15th relief. Took dinner & supper in camp. Stayed in camp until late in evening.

Monday, November 16, 1863
Pleasant and warm. Stood on post from four until six then come to camp & got my breakfast. Got my dinner in camp, ate very harty. Found myself almost sick at night. Changed the guard some on account of orderly. Received a letter, one come from L.

Tuesday, November 17, 1863
Cloudy & cold. Found breakfast ready when I got up. John Davison come over to our camp about middle of the forenoon. We had wheat pancakes for dinner & supper & flour gravy. Had a grand visit. He want back just dark. I went down to

cordaroy Road with him.

Wednesday, November 18, 1863
Pleasant & warm. Detailed on fatigue at half past 7. Went over to Brig. Headquarters from there to Division and got some axes, then to the Brig. & then to the picket line & went to chopping. Took it quite easy, got to camp just about dark. Took supper quite late.

Thursday, November 19, 1863
Pleasant & warm. Detailed on Headquarters guard. Picked out for orderly for the Colonel. Has to be on & off every 2 hours. Took a small bite for dinner. Had a very easy time of it. Run around some for the Col. Stayed on all evening. Stayed at my quarters at night.

Friday, November 20, 1863
Pleasant although some cloudy. Got my breakfast & went over to headquaters & relieved the orderly that stood with me. Uncle Ezra was detailed on headquarters guard. I took his place, stood at the quarter masters tent & stole some sugar & salt in the night.

Saturday, November 21, 1863
Stormy & cool. Stood on guard before the Col. Quarters this morning. Relieved about eleven o'clock. Worked at our tent the rest of the day. Received a letter from home. Wrote an hour in the evening. Found our fire place very nice.

None Such, Tenn Nov. 21/63

Dear Parents

I received your kind letter today & was glad to hear from home once more. I have been looking for a letter from you for a week back. As a general thing I calculate to write once a week but I missed last Sunday. I had about made up mu mind you had stoped writing or got negligent.I should have wrote tomorrow if I had not heard from you as I did. It being Saturday night I thought I would improve my time. I want to go over and see John tomorrow. He made us a visit one day this week. One of our boys saw some fellows from his reg't & they sent word to him that I was dead & he come over to our camp the next day. He has a better chance of running around than we do. We have had so much to do that I have been on duty every day of some kind. Building breastworks & corduroy roads & guard duty, has been rather hard since we come here. I come off of headquarter guard today & have been working at my tent. We have got a log house with a fireplace in it. It is a fine affair too, I tell you. We have four occupants in it. One is Ira Loomis, Ezra, myself & James Storms, a stranger to you. I suppose it looks considerable as though we are going to stay here a spell. We are on a regular hogback. Some like Boliver only more so. The watter is nearer but the hill is steeper. We were in the woods but now the woods have disappeared. You can judge how the woods look here by what you saw in Virginia last winter. I should like to see you down here a spell. A visiting you would find things different than you did the other time. Our house we can stand up in & have lots of room especially for soldiers. We can get up in a very small crinapass if we are obliged to. I found a greenback in your last letter bearing date of the eleventh. They look very well to me although there is a small chance of spending it here & maybe it is better for us. We can by of the comisary with an order from a commissioned officer. When we first got here we lived on three quatter rations & a little extra hardtack come very good once in a while. I have received two letters for L one from his folks & one Wm Humphrey. The one from home had five dollars enclosed in it & two postage stamps. It come the night before

John come over to see us. I let him have it. He said he expected his pay soon & he would send some home in the place of it. I suppose it won't make any difference with Mr Davison folks. Johns regiment lays about three[34]

Sunday, November 22, 1863

Pleasant & warm. Took breakfast and got ready for inspection as usual. Took dinner & started to make John a visit. When I got where the 11 Corps was they were not there. Got back to camp about sundown. Rumore of a march.

Monday, November 23, 1863

Pleasant. Woke up and found myself some what sick with the sick headache. Layed abed until noon. Had a shirt, two pair of socks & pants washed. Fight somewhere in the afternoon. Hear the infantry plain.

The Regimental and Company K Muster Rolls, included earlier in this chapter, stated that the Army stayed in one place until November 24th. It was then that they were given their orders to march and Andrew Gale's next few pages of his diary add to the description of the events, including the fighting and taking care of the wounded, after the battle. He was assigned to ambulance duty for the first time.

Tuesday, November 24, 1863

Some stormy through the day. Ordered to march. Started before breakfast. Crossed the Wauhatchee river on to Lookout mountain at the foot & drove the rebs some three miles & were relieved. Layed on our arms all night.

---

[4] The paper was full and the letter ended there

125

Wednesday, November 25, 1863

Pleasant & warm. The stars and stripes wave on the lookout (cheers). Started off of Lookout mountain about eleven o'clock, arrived at Missionary Ridge just at night. Quite heavy musketry. Whiped them soundly. Took some prisoners & 22 pieces of artilery.

Thursday, November 26, 1863

Pleasant & warm. Started out about eleven o'clock. Moved quite slow through the day. Crossed a small stream just at dark, marched quite late in the evening. Come up pretty close to the rebs. Detailed on picket.

Friday, November 27, 1863

Pleasant & warm. Started on a march about seven o'clock. Crossed the Chickamanga Creek & went to the village of Ringgold. There the Rebs made a stand in the vale and mountain. We drove them fiercly. One man wounded in our company.

Saturday, November 28, 1863

Stormy this morning. Got my breakfast, detailed to go with the wounded. Got them in the ambulance & cars about noon then we took & run them down towards Chattanooga as far as we could on account of some bridges. Received a letter from Mary. Stayed at a house.

Sunday, November 29, 1863

Pleasant & cool. Got some breakfast before daylight. Went back to the cars in the morning. Went to where the wounded were stayed. There all day & night. Buried some seven besides two that were fetched along. Ambulance come at night.

Monday, November 30, 1863

Pleasant but cool. Took breakfast quite early. Got the boys loaded & started off about ten o'clock. Traveled good gog all day. Got to Chattanoga just dark. Got to camp about nine in the evening. Had some cakes for supper.

Gen. Ulyssis S. Grant

Maj. Gen. William T. Sherman

December, 1863 was, for the most part, uneventful according to the records kept by the Regiment. The heavyest fighting was done in the latter days of November. The 137th Regiment assisted in driving the Rebels from atop Lookout Mountain, and had taken position on General Bragg's left flank.

General Ulysis S. Grant, the Union commanding General, was headquartered on Orchard Knob and could overlook the movements of both armies.[35] At sunrise on November 25., General William T. Sherman, began an attack on the Confederate position, but had to halt the operations about noon, when little success had been made.

General Hooker's 20th Corps, which included the 137th Regiment, NYSV, had been delayed at Chattanooga Creek, to repair a burned out bridge, burned by the retreating Rebel Forces. When the finally arrived at the south end of Missionary Ridge, they took the

[35]"Narrative of Military Operations during the Civil War", Gen. Joseph E. Johnston, CSA

ridge quickly, but were of little aid to Gen. Sherman, because of the late hour of the day and the distance they were from him.

The battle carried throught the next day, when the Northern Army, again drove the Southern troops from the ridge and General Bragg's army was broken and in retreat.

Tuesday, December 1, 1863.
Pleasant & cool. Took breakfast before daylight. Expected to go off but did not. The boys that started for the Regt come back. The Regiment come back to camp in the afternoon the drum corps went to meet them. Wrote a letter home received one also.

Wednesday, December 2, 1863
Pleasant. The sun shines fine & warm this morning. Stayed in camp all day. Oscar Myres come to our camp today. Talk of staying with a spell. He and I took a walk down to the battery long towards night. Wrote a letter to mary.

Thursday, December 3, 1863
Pleasant & warm. Inspection today by General Hunter.[36] Had quite a jaunt. Had to go down beyond Gen. Geries headquatters.[37] Stayed around, did not get back until around two o'clock. Had somepancakes for dinner. O Myers is with us.

Friday, December 4, 1863
Pleasant & warm. Ezra is detailed on picket. I received two

---

[6]Gen. David Hunter, USA. Brigade Commander

[7]Gen. John W. Geary, USA. Division Commander under Gen. Hooker.

letters & some yarn. One from home and one from uncle
Nathan. Layed around camp all day. Had quite an Irish dish for
supper. Fixed our tent some today.

Saturday, December 5, 1863
Pleasant & warm. Went down to the Division comisaries to
get some flour. Couldn't get any. Come & got some hardtack
at the Brigade. Detailed to build a guard house in the
afternoon. Over to camp about dark.

Sunday, December 6, 1863
Pleasant & warm. Myers & I started on a tramp about 8
o'clock a.m. We went down in Lookout Valley on the
battlefield got back about noon. Fixed our bed, wrote a letter
to uncle Nathan & sent a note home. Bought some tobacco.

Monday, December 7, 1863
Pleasant & warm. Detailed on fatigue duty. Myers &
Storms out of our tent, also worked on the guard house at
Brigade headquatters all day. Had the headache most of the
day. Drew three days rations. Come to camp before night.

Tuesday, December 8, 1863
Stormy rained all day. Myers & Storms on detail today.
Come in about two o'clock & wrote a letter to Augusta &
Mother. Had some beef for supper. Played eucre some through
the day. Slept very well.

Raccoon Mt. Dec. 8th/63 Dear Sister
I received your letter some time ago but have neglected to
answer it until now. You must excuse me this time & I will try
to do better next time. Today is rather stormy so I thought I
would devote my time to writing a few letters. I live in a log
house with a cloth roof. This winter we have got a fireplace in

our house so we are quite comfortable although it is not like the winters up north. We haven't seen any snow here yet & I am sure I don't care about seeing much this winter. Tell Mother I should been quite happy to of been at home when the girls are out to Groton a visiting from Fleming. I received an invitation from the girls to meet them at our house but it came to late. Tell Grandma I can't tell wheather uncle Ezra will come home or not. He probably will if he can get a furlough & the rhumor is that furloughs are to be granted this winter. I am glad to hear that Scott feels so nice but I think it would full as safe for him to keep off Jack if he knows when he is safe. I send my love to you & the rest of the family. Write soon & oblige your brother.

Andrew

Dear Mother

I received your kind letter some time ago but have neglected to answer it before now but when I write to one of the family it must do for all of you. You spoke of a discharge in your last letter. Discharges have played out. Ezra has got better since I wrote & I am well except a cold. If furloughs are granted probably Ezra will try & come home. I hardly think I shall get home this winter. I don't see much of a chance of a fellow getting home anyway until the war is ended. I come through safe in this last fight. I have seen fighting enough. I wish this thing would close soon. Things look quite favorable here. Old Bragg got pretty badly whiped out last month. In my last I told father he might send me a box if he thought best. If he sends it he better send it as near as possible. Ezra has got his socks & I have got the shirt. No socks has come yet & some other things has not come that I have been looking for. If you would do up things in news papers. I mean you could send things cheaper. I have sent for a razor. Do it up in the Tribune & it will come through for 2 cents. It is getting

most dark & this sheet is most full so I will close hoping this will find you all well.   Write soon & oblige your son,
                                                        Andrew

                              Dec. 9th, 1863
          Dear Father   I received
a few   lines from you in Augustas & Mothers letters. I like to
hear from home ofter & I intend write often in return.
Sometimes it will be a week before I can get a chance to write.
I am on fatigue duty today to be ready to start at fifteen
minutes after seven. Ezra is on guard duty today. I suppose I
will have a trip up on Lookout Mountain today. Yesterday it
rained most all day. It is cloudythis morning but don't rain.
There are a few things at home I would like to have stratened
up & so does uncle Ezra. He says you need not pay John
Shrapstein any thing for he thinks he has got his pay. He thinks
the oats has paid him up. And there is something else. I want to
know how it stands. That is the harness affair. Ezra sayes he
thought that it went in in your last settlement on the buggy. He
sayes you can do as you please about paying Barett when you
please. Let me know how the thing stands. I must close I will
give Ezra a chance to write if he chooses. No more this time.
Please write soon & oblige your son & soldier boy.
                              A. H. Gale
          to
P. B. Gale

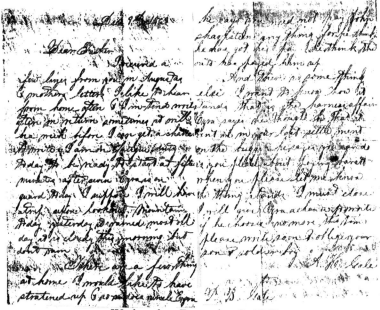

Wednesday, December 9, 1863
Cloudy but not stormy. This morning Ezra detailed on headquatters guard myself on fatigue. Went on Lookout Mountain to build a road. I took love easy. Went up on the point lookout & took a view of the surrounding country. Got in at dark

Thursday, December 10, 1863
Pleasant & warm. Detailed on head quatters guard. Myers on fatigue. Storms also. Had some johnny cakes for breakfast. Acted Corporal of the guard on the second relief. Drew five days rations just at night. Drew a shirt & a pair of pants. Ezra a shirt & drawers.

Friday, December 11, 1863
Pleasant but cool. Relieved from guard about half past nine. Uncle Ezra is on guard today. Had some pancakes for dinner, they were good. I took my bed down & fixed it over. Worked until almost dark. Had quite a pleasant time in the evening.

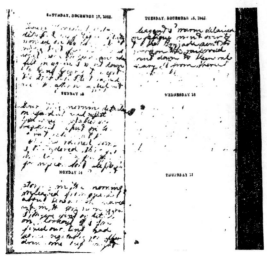
Andrew Gale Diary

Saturday, December 12, 1863
Lousy through the day. Detailed on fatigue duty. Worked on the Sargent Major's tent. Fell in line about noon to hear some orders. Fell in again & went down to Gen. Geary's to escort the 29th N. Y. Regt. Rained all of themseelves afternoon. Did not work.

Sunday December 13, 1863
Lousy this morning. Detailed on guard at headquatters. Had some vegetables for breakfast. Put on the first relief at the spring. Rained some & thundered through the day. Got a few things for my comfort. Slept in my tent.

Monday, December 14, 1863
Stormy in the morning. Relieved from guard abour ten o'clock. Cleared up for the afternoon. Ezra & Myers wemt on detail on lookout & I fixed our tent. Had some vegetables for supper. Drew some beef tonight.

Tuesday, Dec 15, 1863

Pleasant & warm. Detailed on fatigue. Went over to the Brigade, sent to work on the railroad. Went down to General Geary & from there to Lookout Creek than up towards Whitesides & got out ties in the afternoon.

Wednesday, Dec 16, 1863

Pleasant & warm. Started early to work on the railroad. Carried ties in the forenoon. Took dinner, got orders to report to the Brigade. Come into camp and stayed there all the rest of the day Rained hard in the night. Received a letter from lock.

Thursday, December 17, 1863.

Lousy & cool. Tried to cook some beans for breakfast. Couldn't get them done so had to go with a cold bite. Built a cordaroy road. Quit about middle of the afternoon & come to camp. Went out on picket to see Ezra. He felt quite smart, more so than (gusto)

Friday, December 18, 1863

Pleasant & cool. Detailed to work on the road that goes to the landing. Our Regt built 100 yds of cordaroy, got through little after noon. Went after some soft bread but got none. Got to camp about three, found a hotcake Drew two days ration of beef.

Saturday, December 19, 1863

Pleasant this morning but chilly. Detailed on the road again. Had some liver for breakfast, went down to Geary's to grind an ax. Went into the comassary & got some sugar & hardtack or Myers did. The 66 Ohio went home today. Ezra come in from picket.

Sunday, December 20, 1863

Pleasant & cold. Not very well this morning. My head aches some. Did not come out on inspection. Storms is on headquatters guard. Stayed in camp all day. Washed my neck & shaved. Drew three days rations, wrote two letters in the evening, one home one another to Mary.

Sunday, Dec. 20th/63

Dear Parents

I hardly think I am owing you a letter although I suppose you would like to hear from me & I should like to hear from you as much. It has been about a month since I have heard from you. I have not received any stamps from home lately. We are still on the hogback that we encamped on when we first came here. We were all of lasr week at work on the railroad & on the wagon road to the river. The road has been so bad we had to live on three quatters rations. If it had not been for the money you sent me, we should have had to went hungry a good many times. We get once in a while a hotcake & they go very well for soldiers to eat. Anything that is good enough for a nigger is good enough for a soldier. It is about as the nigger says in the army there was a nigger enlisted. He sayed they promised him all kinds of good things & as soon as they got him fast he was no better than a white man. That is about the feeling of the black varments. I don't like the nigger much better than I did at home. I think my love for them diminished some since I have been amongst them. You must have some chilly weather up your way. The reason is when the wind is in the north it is rather raw & cold. It has been frosty nights of late, about as cold as Oct. in York state. There has not been any snow here yet. I should like to be at home about New Years to eat dinner with you. There is some talk of our division going to recruit but I don't have much hope of out going. There has regiments enlisted & gone home &

several more intend to soon. Our division will be very small after the two year men enlist. There will not be enough for a whole regiment hardly in our Division. If we should come home I would be a tickled chap I reckon. I have not received those socks yet. I want you to send me some papers. I received a Dryden News last week. I suppose it come from you. The Eleventh Corps come back to Chattanooga last week. I have not seen John yet. If I am not on duty tomorrow I think I will go over & see him but I am on duty most of the time. The report is too that Hooker is going to take the 11 & 12 Corps along with him. There are all sorts of stories in the Army. No more this time. Write soon & oblige your son & soldier boy. Give my love to all.   A. H. Gale

Monday, December 21, 1863
Pleasant & Cool. Detailed on guard. Half froze in the shade all day. Was on before the Colonels quatters, stayed at the guard house most of the time. Ezra on guard also.He was at the spring. Considerably warmer towards night.

Tuesday, December 22, 1863
Pleasant & warm today. Relieved about ten o'clock. Had some beans for dinner, rather a slim supper. Crocker cut a good pile of night wood. Set up & boiled some beans. Ezra went out on the picket line and got an order on the commassary.

Wednesday, December 23, 1863
Cloudy & cool. Got up before daylight. No duty today. Got some grapes over to the Brigade. Done a little washing for myself. Fixed the tent some in the afternoon. Had some beans for supper. Grew quite cold in the afternoon. Sat up quite late.

Thursday, December 24, 1863

Pleasant & cool. Detailed on Headquatters guard. Had some biscuits. Two in number for my dinner & some hardtack. Come over to camp in the evening & got my supper. Stayed until about ten o'clock. Stood one trick in the night, some cold. Received a diary Christmas eve.

Friday, December 25, 1863

Cloudy & cool. Relieved from guard about ten o'clock. Had some beans, onions and hardtack for my Christmas dinner. Storms is on guard from our tent. Got some of my clothes washed by Mrs.Fanning. Wrote a letter to uncle Nathan in Ezras letter.

Saturday, December 26, 1863

Rainy & cool. Ezra was detailed on guard. I stayed around in camp all day. Cleaned up my gun. It took most of the day. Long towards night went over to the Brigade goot some meal & fresh hogs liver & heart. Received two letters, one from home. Stormed in night.

Sunday, December 27, 1863

Cloudy & foggy. Had some liver for breakfast, also some hotcakes. Had inspection as usual. Stormed most of the day. I boiled some tongue & hart. Stayed in my tent most of the day. Wrote two letters. One home. Ezra had the headache.

Sunday Dec. 27th/63

Dear Father

I received your long looked for letter last week. I had begun to think that you never intend to write to me again. I guess you don't answer more than half my letters. If you do they don't come. This one bears date Dec. 13. I received a diary Christmas eve. It come quicker

138

than I expected. I am very thankful for it. I intend sending my old one home but I don't know as it will hardly pay to pay the postage & another thing I don't want old Jay peaking into it. I sent another paper home a spell ago with some trinkets in it. I suppose the old puke will open them if he can,t behave himself. I'll send my letter to some other post office. In your last letter there were eight stamps & a fifty cent note which come very exceptable. My money nearle played out & my stamps all. I am in hopes we will get payed before long. Uncle Sam is owing me fifty odd dollars. We are gooing back towards Nashville. I suppose in a day or two. The report is that we are going to Stevenson, Alabama probably to winter if we get along the railroad. A box would come to me in a little while. In my other letter I wrote for you to send me a box to Chattanooga. I am in hopes you have not sent yet. If not, I will tell you im my next where to send it. It is raining here today. It has rained for a day or two now. There is no snow here yet. Quite an oopen winter, more so than I am used to seeing. We have had pleasant weather most of the time since we have been here. There is not much going on here at present. Only most of the old troops are enlisting over again. They got a chance to go home thirty days by enlisting but it wouldent pay me to stay three years longer for a thirty day furlough. I should like to come home very well & maybe we will get a chance. The Capt. that is in command of the regiment says he is trying to get our regiment home too recruit sixty or ninety days. If he succeeds, which I think is doubtful, I will try & make old Groton a call. No more this time. I send Mother, the children. Grandma & yourself my love. Please write soon and oblige your son & soldier boy.

Andrew H. Gale   P.S. Pa Pa

to his, this leaves me well with a full belly. Ezra is well also. In your next let us know how much you got for pony & all the news (Wheather you have paid Harve as I wanted you to.)

Monday, December 28, 1863

Cloudy & cool. Had nothing to do but eat. The Regiment went to Gearys to see a fellow drummed out of camp. No one went from our tent but Storm drew three days rations of bread, some beef & pork. Cooked some beans in evening.

Tuesday, December 29, 1863

Pleasant & warm. Nothing to do today. Had some beef & indian cakes for breakfast. Had inspection in the afternoon at three o'clock by some of Gen. Gearys staff. Got through before night. Went in Halletts tent in the evening.

Wednesday, December 30, 1863

Pleasant but cloudy. Detailed on picket about noon to relieve the 102nd. We went on the lookout post. Come to camp & got my supper. It consisted of fried beef & vegetables. The boys went down to the orders for muster. Rained most of the night.

Thursday, December 31, 1863

Stormy & cool. Rained most of the day. Stayed on the mountain all day. Got some wet. Fixed our house so it kept the rain off pretty well. Stood on post from half past six til half past eight then layed down for the night. Slept very well most of the time although it was pretty cold. Snowed a considerable through the night. The cold weather we have had this winter. New Years morning. Relieved from picket. The ground looks white with snow & a cold wind. Good fall weather for York state.

This is the end of the hand written entries by Andrew H. Gale, entered into his diary during the year 1863. At this writing, no 1862 diary has been located and only two pages from his 1864 diary have been found. What is learned, regarding Andrew's activities, have come from these two pages and letters written by him to members of his family at home.

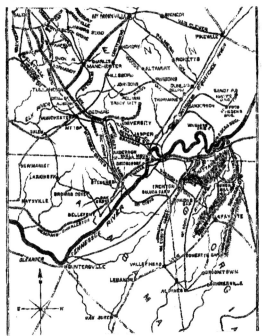

Most of the diary entries, thus far included, were written in pencil and in a very legible penmenship. There were pages, here and there, that were entered by ink pen.

Prior to July 14, in the time segment covered so far, all of the diary entrys were made while Andrew was home in Groton. He spent that time at home recovering from an illness he contracted, while on duty with the Army, in Virginia. He also spent considerable time doing farm chores for his father, and enjoying civilian life, while at home.

Andrew Gale made two attempts to rejoin his Regiment, before being successful. This took him from June 22, 1863 until July 27, 1863. A total of one month and five days. From that time on, Andrew H. Gale was again a soldier, fighting for a country he believed in.

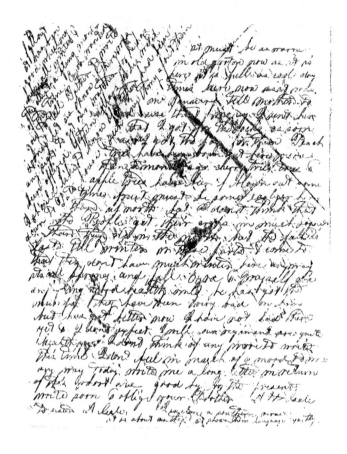

A different Style of Letter Writing

Chapter Eight

The fighting in November led to a quiet month of December for the 137th Regiment and the remainder of the 20th Corps. It was spent at camp near Wauhatchie, Tenn., where fatigue duties were performed and much needed rest was taken by the men of the Regiment.

January of 1864, saw the first movement in almost a month. The Regimental and Company records, again give a very descriptive picture.

From the Field & Staff Muster Roll:
Jan. & Feb. 1864   Stevenson, Ala-Feb. 29, 1864
The Regt. left Wauhatchie on the 4th day of Jan. 1864 marching to Whiteside, bivouacking for the night at 8 P.M. Started on the morning of the 5th, arriving at Bridgeport, Ala. About 3 o'clock, P.M., left Bridgeport at 5 A.M. on the morning of the 6th arriving at Stevenson, Ala. 4 o'clock P.M. on the same day. Since which time six companies of the Regt have been doing Provost Guard duty. The remaining 4 companies being engaged in doing guard duty and escorting prisoners to their respective Regts in the various Corps in this Dept. Drills and dress parades have been held daily.

The Company K Muster Roll repeats much the same as above.

Jan & Feb 1864 Stevenson, Ala.
On the 4th day of January we broke camp at Wauchatchie, Tenn and marched in a westerly direction. A three day march brought us to Stevenson, Ala. A distance of 34 miles. Here we have since remained doing Provost Duty.

Although only a few pages of diary were found, for 1864, Andrew Gale wrote letters home telling his parents, just what was happening with him and the boys in the regiment.

In a January letter to his father, at home in Groton, N.Y., Andrew is fascinated by the spring like weather he was experiencing in the South. This was unique to a farm boy raised in central New York state.

Jan 23/64

Dear Father

I received your kind note two or three days ago & it come very exceptable. I assure you we are still at Stevenson & we have made vast difference you bet since we have been here. We don't have to work any. The guard house generally is pretty well filled up & when there is any work to be done, they have to do it & we guard them while they work. It is very fine weather here. It seems like summer, the sun shines, warm, the ground is dry & if was a farmer I should be plowing I think. I have not seen any box yet but hope it will come along soon. I shall send to Chattanooga for it the fore part oof next week if I don't see it before. I understand that the U States are trying to raise a million of men to go into Richmond. I hope it is so. I think is rather a slim chance for getting home this winter. We don't hear anything like furloughs down here. I am glad you sold your corn so well. I wish I had some of your apples about now. They cost so like fun here. I can hardly afford to eat them. This leaves me well & I hope this epistle will find you also. From   Andrew to his Pa.

Dear Mother
I take this opportunity to answer your kind note you wrote me. I am always glad to hear from home at all times & like to have them come often. I have plenty to eat now & am perfectly

contented if we can only stay here. If you could stay one winter in the southern region, especially as far down as I am, you would see a different sort of winter than you ever wittnessed before. I received the socks you sent me. I am looking for the box you sent me every day. No more this time. I give my love to the children & Grandma & a sufficient quanity yourself. This is from you son.

Andrew to his Ma Chloe

Sent my last years portfolio home yesterday. Don't let everyone be looking in to it. Take care of it for me & oblige me.

A. H. Gale

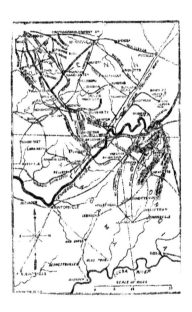

Andrew's last paragraph, in this letter, gives an insight into how the letters and diaries, of the soldiers, arrived in the hands of the families at home. He relates about sending his "portfolio" for 1863, home. That portfolio included all of the letters received from family and friends, as well as the diary he kept through out the year.

Stevenson   February 14th/64

Dear Cousin

I received your letter last week and the verses. They are very nice. Your letter found me well & I hope these few lines will find you enjoying the same blessing. I am up to Ezra's tent while I write. It has been trying to rain every since morning but it can't hardly make it out yet. It has been very nice weather here of late. Little boys running around bare footed. It seems the most like Sunday today it has since I left home. I suppose you have meetings Sunday night at the little red school house as of old. Ezra is on guard today. This place is some larger that West Groton & nearly as large as Milan. There is more business done here than in a dozen such places. The railroad runs through here. There is some six or eight engines in here most of the time & it is nothing to see over a hundred cars here at a time. They are a whistle all times of night & day. I have got some more letters to write so I will bid you good bye for this time. Give my love to all of your folks & keep a good place yourself. Write soon & oblige your affectionate cousin

Shelton   Andrew

Dear Sister

I have answered Sheldons letter, now I will address a few lines to you supposing you to be looking for an answer also. I am well & enjoying myself fine. We are still in our old fosish at Stevenson yet. I wish I could buy things was as cheap here as they are in Groton. Eggs are five cents a piece here and other things to match. Match puts me in mind of Ann & the young cook. I wonder if that match will take flow in the spring, hope so. May be then he will mind his own business then. I am in hopes those apples will get down this way by & by. Hope they will come quicker than the other box for I have not seen any thing of it yet. I am going to send to Nashville this week by our comasary sargent & see if it is there. You spoke of cold weather. It has been dusty every since we have been here until today, the pleasantest winter I ever saw. I don't think of any more to write this time. Please excuse me this time. Write soon & oblige your affectionate Brother. Give my love to all & keep a good share yourself. No more this time.

Andrew
To
Augusta

Dear Father

      I received your letter last part of last week. It has been some lousy today so I thought I would write you a few lines to inform you that I was well. I received six stamps in your letter. They always come acceptable. I understand that a great many are emlisting. I am glad the North have such an intrest in this war & I am in hopes it will wind up this summer. I suppose you have begun to think some of moving by this time. I should like to be there to help you. I don't have much to do & that suits me to a dot. I was rather a lazy boy. Soldiering is just the business for lazy folks. We got two months pay day before yesterday, all in cash. I think I shall keep my money this time. I don;t like to send for it. The veterans have commenced returning. They have been going home very fast for the past month. I should like a furlough but not three years more for thirty days of liberty. I am tired of writing. I have written considerable today. I remain your obedient son.   Andrew Gale

To his Pa

Ezra & I have sent some things in paper to West Groton. I want you to get them. I wrote in one of my others who they were for. I thought I would get them out of the hands of old Jay.

The Field & Staff records that corresponded with the letters included above, also show a lull in the fighting activities of the 137th Regiment. Referring, again, to the military records of the Regiment and the Company, the following transpired during March and April of 1864

Field & Staff Muster Roll
March & Apr. 1864   Stevenson, Ala.   April 30, 1864
Since the muster of Feb 29the the Regt has remained at Stevenson, Ala during which it has been doing Provost Guard duty, camp and Brigade guard duty and fatigue work on the various fortifications. Drills, squad, Company & Battallion have been held.Schools for commissioned and non commissioned officers have been held whenever practicabley and guard mounting and dress parades have been ommitted excepting in inclement weather. The health of the men of the Regt was never better than at the present time.

The Company K Muster Roll had no entry for these two months other than the date and location, Stevenson, Ala.

March 1, 1864
Dear Father
Well I finally got that long looked for box. It come last Saturday. The things were a great deal better than I supposed. They were nothing spoilt at all. Some of the cookies were tainted, the sausilage was a little moldy on the outside but it tastes first rate. There was nothing disturbed at all. Myers got his box the same day that I did mine. We are still at Stevenson.

Today it is some stormy, the weather. Last month was warm & dry. The dust flies most of the time like a windy day in August. My health has been very good since I come down here. It is healthier here than it is in old "Virginia", the water is very good as far as I have been this way. There is no way of ascertaining the weight of letters & papers. The Post Office is a kind of one horse machine. The Office is not more than ten or fifteen rods from my quatters. I don't have much to do now but I am some lazy I notice & since my box come, I have lived like an officer. Myers got about as much butter as there was in one of the pails. We get new bread every morning so we have bread & butter all the time. I have got over my cold. I would like to be home. I could tell you more than I can write. I am glad you got those watches although they are higher priced than I wanted. John has not got to the regt. yet but I guess they will come safe after all. This is an awful place for speculation a fellow was only his own boss. The talk is that the soldiers are going to have their wages raised somewhere from sixteen to twenty five dollars a month. I don't care if they do raise our wages a little at least I have no objections. I don't think of any more to write any more this time. Write soon & oblige your son & soldier boy.

A. H. Gale

Dear Sister

I received your welcome not some days ago. I am so lazy now days that I can hardly afford to eat after the vituals are on the table. I should like to be at home & see the folks but it wouldent hardly pay to come home & stay a day or two & then come right back. We have got the privilege of conversing by way of letter & I am thankful for that. No more this time. Write soon.

From Andrew

March 16th/64

Dear Father

I received your kind note bearing date March the 8th & was very glad to hear from you once more & to hear the folks were well. I am enjoying exceeding good health now days. We are still at Stevenson. We get rumors that we are going to leave very often. We can't put much dependance in army reports. The paper states that General Grant is again in Nashville, I suppose on business. I hear that General Smith is in command of the Army of the Potomac. I hope they will get someone in there by & by that will suit them. There are soldiers passing through most every day to the front.I rather guess that Uncle Sam is going to do something this summer at least I hope so. The stamps you sent come very exceptable. I was nearly out. There seems to be quite a change in our neighborhood this spring. I should like to be home a spell this spring to help you move. Nothing would suit one better but I can't always have my wish in all things. We must be content with our lot here on earth. We are having rather a cold snap here just about now. It has been quite cool here for two or three days but today is the coldest yet. It rather pinches us up to have a cold snap, it being so warm when it is pleasant. I received a letter from Frank Gale this week. They were well. I have something I would like to send home if we move from here. I will try & express a box home one of these days. You need not send me any more boxes this winter. Those watches have not made their appearance yet. John has not got back yet & Pat Fanning had some hints from home that he never will come back. Pat thinks that he has gone to the old country. I hardly think he has. If he has, away goes the watches. I have not much to write this time. I send my love to all. Write soon and oblige your son & soldier boy.

Andrew H. Gale

Thursday, Apr. 19th, 1864

Dear Sister

I received your letter & Fathers yesterday bearing the date the 10th & was glad to hear from home once more. It had been quite a good while since I heard from you & I almost had a mind to think you had forgotten me but I suppose our folks have been very busy of late moving. I am glad to hear they have got their place. I expect Mother will take comfort now.She has been waiting a home of her own so long. I got those socks the same time I did the letter & sold them today. Tell Father to send me some stamps in his next. We are still in Stevenson. The Eleventh Corps and ours are to be consolidated & called the Twentieth Corps & commanded by General Hooker. There were six regiments of Ill. Troops passed through here last week. All new regiments, lately got up. Two big guns went through here on the cars. They weighed almost five tons a piece. They carried a hundred pound shot & had a seven bore. You bet they were something of a gun. U. S. Has everything to cause destruction to life. The weather has been rather unpleasant of late, raining most of the time but in two days it will be dry and nice. The ground don't have frost enough for the bottom to fall out. It has been good wheeling here all winter & the dust a flying most of the time. Ezra wanted you to tell Father to write soon & let us know if there was any sight to get our watches for he has been offered fifteen dollars for his watch. I should like to know if Father has been down to Pats house & seen anything about them. It must be as warm in old Groton now as it is here. It is full as cool day times here now as it was in January. Tell Mother to use that money I send her that I got for the socks. As soon as I get pay for them. Peach trees have boarn out here more than a month ago. Cherry trees & apple trees have been blown out some time. Fruit must be some earlyr here than up north but I don't think that the people get their crops in much

151

sooner than they did in the north but the fall is lasts till winter in these parts & come to that they don't have much winter here anyway. Its all spring & fall. Ezra & myself are enjoying good health only he has got the mumps. They have been very bad on him but he got better now. I have not had them yet & I don't expect I will. Our regiment are quite healthy. I don't think of any more to write this time. I don't feel in much of a mood to write any way today. Write me a long letter in return of this short one. Good by for the present. Write soon & oblige your Brother.

A. H. Gale To Sister Augusta

Enclosed a southern verse. It is about as they it shows them language exactly.

Forest Church, Georgia
May 6th, 1864

Dear Parents

As Ezra has been teasing me for several days to write a few lines to inform you that we had sent a box home by express to Courtland. I sent a blanket, the holes through was caused by the bullit I sent home. I sent a razor & a pair of gloves, a knife & fork for Augusta also a razor strap. Ezra sent a coat, a needle book & contents a razor & some books. The lightest rubber blanket belongs to him, the other to me. I think that is all there is in the box. Well we have been on the march since last Monday. We are not far from Ringold & not far from Dalton, the rebels stronghold. I have stood the march very well all but my feet. They are some sore. We are lying still most of the day today. We marched about four miles this morning. I saw John Davison today. He is in our Corps now in the Third Division. We are no more the twelth Corps but the Twentieth Corps. We have four Divisions now. One (the Fourth Division) are on the railroad or was the last I heard from them. We are commanded by Hooker. John is well and looks tough. He smashed his toe some time ago & it has not got well yet. Ezra & myself are well. It is very pretty country through here. The corn is up & winter wheat is all most headed out. The crops in general look well. The land through here would suit you. There is not a stone large enough to throw at a bird. You must excuse a short letter this time. I have been waiting a long time to get a letter from home but have been sadly disappointed this long time. I got a letter from Frank Gale yesterday morning, while at Chattanooga. It is almost night & I must close for this time. I ever remain you son & soldier boy. With much love.

My love to all the children   Andrew H. Gale

May 20th/64

Dear Parents

I have an opportunity to send a letter so I am improving the time. We are lying still or have been this fore noon. Since I wrote last he have had some hard marching & this army has had some pretty hard fighting but our regiment has been very lucky thus far. I have not fired my gun yet but last Sunday we were where the bullet come pretty thick. There was four wounded in our regiment, none killed. Our Corps lost heavily especially the third division. They had to charge a fort. They drove the Rebs back but they could not hold it nor could the Rebs. Sunday night they retreated & we have been chasing them ever since. Yesterday our third division had a brush with the Johnnies and took eight pieces of artillary. It is very warm here now. The farmers have been cultivating their corn. Potatoes are good size, strawberries are getting ripe, peaches are as large as hickory nuts. Ezra & myself are doing finely. You can see by looking on the map about where we are While I am writing it is on the railroad that runs from Dalton to Atlanta. I think this country would suit you pretty well. Some places there are no

153

stone at all. There is a great deal more woodland than I supposed. There was until I had a tramp in there parts. We are quite a piece from Stevenson now. We have been travelling for nearly three weeks. I would like to have you send some papers occassionaly for we don;t get any news now at all. I don;t think of any more this time. Please excuse all mistakes & bad writing. My love to all. Write soon and oblige son & soldier boy.

A. H. Gale

Georgia, Wednesday, A.M. June 2nd/64

Dear Parents

The Chaplain said this morning we had a chance to send out letters today so I thought I would write a few lines home to let you know that I am in the land of the living. We have been marching & fighting ever since we come into Georgia. We were relieved by the fifthteenth corps yesterday. We were in the breastworks & had been them a week or more picking away at each other. Out regiment has been very lucky thus far. We have only lost one man in our company since we left Stevensn by bullets. That was Stoddard of Groton. He was wounded. There has been only fourteen casualities in the regiment. We are not far from a town called Dalas & not far from Marietta. We lay in the woods now. We marched about four miles after we were relieved & stoped for the night. It is mostly woods where we have been traveling of late. Ezra & myself are well. We are some fatigued by being disturbed of our rest most every night. There would be firing on our left and then we would pile out of bed & get ready for the Johnnies but they didn't come up to our breastworks at all. If they had they would of got some cold lead. I reckon they seem to be very reluckant a bout retreating any further towards Atlanta. I have nothing more of consequence to write this time. I should not of wrote today only to let you know that we were well. If I was at home I could talk off quite a letter. Please excuse all mistakes & short epistle. Write soon & oblige your son & soldier boy.

A. H. Gale

June 8 /64

Lost Mt., Ga.

Dear Parents

As I have some liesure time today I thought I would write a few lines home although I have not heard from you in nearly a month. We are lying behind some breastworks now but I guess the Johnnies are a few & smattering in front. The report is that they have retreated acrost the river. We were in the breastworks near Dalas a week. The Rebs breastworks & ours were not more than forty if they were thirty rods apart & our rifle pits were about eight to ten rods in front of our breast-works & if a Reb showed himself a bullet was sure to go after him & it was the same with us. The sixtieth N. York lost a good many men before the rifle pits were made. Our regiment has not lost more than fourteen or fifteen men yet, killed & wounded. Some regiments have lost nearly two hundred. Stoddard is the only man hurt in our company. There has been three sent to the hospital of sickness since we started. Ezra & myself are well & tough yet. I don't know as my health was ever better although I was never sick when I was at home. We come here where we lay night before last. We built breast works most all day yesterday. Today we are to have inspection at three o'clock. It is very warm weather here now days. It seems to agree with me very well. The boys in general are healthy. One thing the watter is very good in this country. It would suit you to a dot here in Georgia. There are thousands of acres of ground here without a stone & then some places it is all stone. There is a great deal more woodland here than I expected there was.[38] Everything is very forward here. Apples are large enough to stew. I think peaches will be ripe by the fourth. Strawberries have been ripe some time, corn is nearly knee high & hansomer pieces of wheat I never saw than we passed through on our march. Some was as high as my head & very thick & the soil seem to be rich where ever we go & everything looks prosperous. It is laid out for the government to think of starving the south to terms for they can raise better crops or as good as the people of the north. I hope I shall hear from you by & by. I have wrote ofter but get very few answers. I don't think anything more to write this time. Please excuse all mistakes & bad writing. Write soon and oblige your son & soldier boy.

Andrew H. Gale

The May Muster Roll of the 137th Regimental Clerk had no entry. It was simply dated and signed from New Hope Church, Ga. However, the Field & Staff Muster Roll included a short description of the May and June activities, of the regiment and one most important piece of information to the writing of this book. Information pertaining specifically to Andrew H. Gale, the young 24 year old farmer volunteer from Groton, New York.

The months of May and June, 1864, saw the 137th Regiment, N.Y.S.V., begin taking serious casualties for the first time since the battle of Gettysburg.

Field & Staff Muster Roll
May & June 1864 Near Marietta, Ga.
June 30, 64 Broke camp at Stevenson, Ala.,

---

[38]This fasinated Andrew Gale, as he mentioned these statements in previous lett•

May 2nd 1864. Reached Bridgeport same evening. 3rd regt started camping at Shell Mound. Left Shell Mound morn of 4th reaching Chattanooga 9 P.M. Started from Chattanooga on the 5th marching day after day until we reached Resaca, Ga. where we became engaged with the enemy on the 15th of May. Reg't losing 1 Officer & five men wounded.

June 1 lost 2 men wounded on skirmish line. June 17th near Marietta, Ga. Had 1 man killed & 1 wounded while taking up position. 21st, 2 men wounded on skirmish line, 22nd, 1 man killed, 1 Officer & 3 men wounded. 28th, 1 man wounded by shell. June 30th found us still near Marietta, Ga. Whole distance marched 230 miles.

The Company K, Muster Roll has recorded as follows:
May & June 1864   Near Marietta, Ga.

On the 2nd day of May, 1864, this Company with the 137th   Regt, N.Y.V. broke camp at Stevenson, Ala. And with the 20th Corps moved to join Sherman's[39] Army then in front of Dalton, Ga. It was engaged at the battle of Resacca, Ga. and in nearly all the subsequent battles of the campaign up to June 30 which found us in the trenches in front of the enemy who were there in line of battle with their right resting on Kenesaw Mt. near Marietta, Ga.

The Field & Staff Muster Roll list the casualties for June and specifically mentions the date of June 22 and 1 man killed. That one man was Andrew H. Gale.

Although Andrew's 1864 Diary was never returned to the family, or has not shown up in a family trunk, as has his Diary of 1863,

---

[9]Brig. Gen. William Tecumseh Sherman, commanding General of all Union Armies in the Western Sector.

a short note from the Regimental Chaplain and two pages of the 1864 Diary were available at the writing of the book. The note from the Chaplain tells how young Gale died and the few diary pages, from June 1864, tell what it was like during his last few days. Records from the National Archives, give June 22 as the date on which Andrew Gale was killed, but the six days of diary entries , in June of 1864, show an entry for the 22nd and the note written by Chaplain E. F. Roberts, is dated June 24, 1864.

The following are the last six days in the life of Andrew H. Gale, 137th Regiment, N.Y.S.V

Friday, June 17, 1864

Cloudy but warm in the morning. Ordered under arms at daylight. *No Rebs to be found this morning very close. Took* breakfast in the rebels breastworks. They had very good works. We went on the east side of Lost Mountain. Started about eleven o'clock. Went about a mile & formed in lines of battle. They tried to shell us. Drove them about a mile. There wea quite an artilery duel in the afternoon. We drible quicked across a place where the Rebs had a rake & killed & wounded some three or four. None in our company. We built breastworks most of the night. Got two letters from home.

Saturday, June 18, 1864

Commenced raining about daylight & rained all day. There was skirmishing and cannonading all day. I shot off my gun at a gray back. Could see them running back & forth from an old house in front our breastworks. Was on the lookout from nine until eleven. Drew rations of (unreadable)

Sunday, June 19, 1864

Stormy again this morning. The Johnny Rebs have skedatled again. Pretty muddy under foot. Drew liquor again this morning. Started on the march at nine. Went sometime two miles & found the enemy entrenched lay in the woods until dark. Our Batteries belted them some first night. We moved after dark & built breastworks. None hurt in our Regiment today.

Monday, June 20, 1864

Cloudy & cool. Skirmishing kept up as usual & occassionaly a shell to keep the Rebs awake. Was relieved about ten. We are some four miles from Marietta. None lost in our Regiment today. Last night we moved, went about half a mile and stoped for the night. Sharp firing near where we left.

Tuesday, June 21, 1864

Cloudy this morning. Stayed out about nine. Went out on the skirmish line. Six companys of our Regiment were out all day.Rained most of the time. At night the other four companys relieved the six. We were out all night. Built rifle pits. The Rebs fell back from their rifle pits on the hill. We advanced on the hill & commenced throwing up fire & they threw over some shells. We fell back over the hill.

Wednesday, June 22, 1864

Pleasant & warm. The Rebs left the hill. We fired some & then advanced & commenced throwing up rails. They throw over a shell or two & we fell back behind the hill.

This is the last diary entry made by Pvt. Andrew H. Gale. The final bit of information, on the life of this young Union soldier, came two short days later, when this hand written note, on a sheet of paper measuring two and three quarter inches by six inches, was attached to his portfolio and sent home, to the Gale family, in Groton, New York.

It read:

Battlefield, Marietta Georgia, June 24, 1864

Mr. P. B. Gale

Dear Sir,   This book and letters with a few found, has been placed in my hands, to send you.

The letter with full details of the sad event which has befallen young Gale goes with the same mail. I most deeply Sympathize with those who morne this boy. We shall also miss him, in the Regiment for he was a true soldier and had gone out on the skirmish line, without the knowledge of his company commander. So anxious was he to end the days of rebels. A sharpshooter picked him off, sending a ball through his head.

Yours in sorrow
E. F. Roberts
Chaplain, 137th, N.Y.

Battlefield Marietta
Georgia June 24th 1864

Mr S. B. Gale,

Dear Sir, This book,
and pen, with a friendly
lines, had been placed in
my hands, to send you.
The letter with full
details, of the sad event
which had befallen
young Gale goes with
the same mail. I must
deeply sympathize with
those who mourn his
loss. We shall also miss
him, in the Regiment.
for he was a true soldier,
and had gone out on the
Skirmish line, without
the knowledge of his com-
pany commander, So
anxious was he To end
the class of rebels. A sharp
shooter picked him off sending a ball through his head.
Yours in Sorrow
E. F. Roberts
Chaplain 127 R. [?]

So ended the life of a young soldier, on the field of battle, in one of the bloodiest and hard fought wars known to mankind. This is just one story in the many thousands like it through out the five long years, to hold the Union of States together.

Although Andrew H. Gale lost his life on the skirmish line, in an action he did not have to be in, according to the letter from the Regimental Chaplain, the 137th Regiment, N.Y.S.V., carried on and Andrew's Uncle Ezra was one of those who had to continue, even though he felt a great loss, in the death of his nephew. Ezra wrote the following letters, to the family back in Groton, N.Y., expressing his grief and loneliness. He also described the continuing action with the enemy as the 137th Regiment advanced through Georgia, as part of the 20th Corps and part of Sherman's Army.

June 29/64
Georgia Camp nigh Marietta

Dear Nice (niece)

I suppose you think I have forgotten you but I have not by no mins (means). I think of you evry day and like to here from you often but the resan (reason) I did not writ oftener, Andrew wrot how I was so I thought there was know youse of my writen but now he is gon and I must writ. I received the letter you and your father sent to Andrew, June 26th. I open it and read it and new that he cod not be here to see the filing (feeling) that you and your folks had for him and me. It fill my heart with sadness and grief. Augusta I can not writ know more this tim. I must clos. Writ son as you get this. Don't forget to writ. I was glad to here that you and Laverna had a good visit and was well. This is from your uncle Ezra Bostwick to my little nice Augusta gal. My love to you & good by.

Dear Brother Peter

I have ben writin
a few lins to Augusta so I though I wold writ you a few lins to
let you know that I was live and well and hopeing thes few lins
will find you all well. We have advenced our lines since I wrot
you last a mile. There was none killed, none woned (wounded)
out of our regiment. We bilt strong breast works and ar laying
behind them wating for them to come. The picets (pickets)
keep up quit hevy firing this morning yet. The canon ar still this
morning. Yesterday the shell flew from both sids thick and
faste. Or canon can sillance theirs. We have got breast works
shell proff. So let them schot (shoot). The papers say that we
have got Marietta but we have not. We ar three miles of
from the place. I think they will get away from there soon.
Ireceived the letter you sent to Andrew, June Sunday 26th. I
opened it and found some stamps. I will keep them and pay
you for them. It was a very lonesome day to me. Peter there is
good thing. Wold like to writ but I don't feel much like writen
this morning. Writ soon   E. B.

July 10th/64

Georgia Camp nigh the river that crosses over to
Atlanta
Dear Brother Peter

I received a letter from you and Augusta and
Mother a week ago and wold have ancerd it befor this but I
have had know tim. The Rebs hav ben falling back evry day
from their strong breast works and we have ben folowing them
up, We hav got then drove acrost the river now. I hope we
may have a little wrest now for a while for we have had long
march and hard tim of it since we left Stevenson. We can see
Atlanta by geting up in a tree. It is 8 or 10 miles of (off). I
received a nother letter from you for Andrew yesterday. The

letter you and Augusta sent before. I found 6 stamps in it. I will keep them and pay you for them. When I read your good letter you sent to Andrew telling him how well you liked your new home and how well your crops look, my filings I can not tell you O how I wish I cod (could) be there with you wonce but that can not be so now if I live I hope the tim will soon com. The wether here has ben very wharm and dry long back. Now Peter I must close my letter. Writ as soon as you get this. I send my love to wone and all. If we get in camp to stay a while I will try to writ ofton and I want you and the wrest of my friend to do the saim for you know that I am very lonsom.

This is from your Brother, Ezra Bostwick

To P. B. Gale   Good by

I believe I wrot to you in wone of my other letters that wanted you to send me a day book. Send it and I will pay you for it.

Since the letters and the diary from Andrew Gale, and his Uncle Ezra Bostwick, are not available from this point on, June 1864, the remainder of the information, regarding the 137th Regiment, was gathered from the already quoted Regimental and Company Records, obtained from the National Archives, in Washington, D. C. These were copied from micro film files and were written by the clerks and Non Commissioned Officers of the Regiment.

The entire transcript of the Field and Staff Muster Rolls were signed by an Officer known only as Lewis. They continue on from the June dates in 1864, as reported in this chapter.

What transpired during the next six to eight months, was all part of the Union Army's march on Atlanta and then Sherman's famous march to the sea. The 20th Corps, of which the 137th Regiment, N.Y.S.V. was a part, was one of the major units of Sherman's Army.

Field & Staff Muster Roll

July & Aug. 1864 Paces Ferry, Ga.   Aug 31, 1864
The first of July found the Regiment still near Marietta, Ga.
July 3rd the enemy evacuated his position encircling Kenesaw
Mountain and at 6:30 A.M. we left the line we had so long
occupied and followed the retreating foes. July 5th we went
into camp on a high ridge and some of the boys by climbing
trees obtained the first view of Atlanta, distant about 10 miles.
After remaining in camp about 10 days we crossed the river on
the 17th day of July and this Regt being in the advance was
deployed as skirmishers. We advanced until we reached Peach
Tree Creek at night. The creek was successfully crossed and on
the 20th, Hood[40] charged the 20th Corps. This Regt.Lost 8
men killed and 21 wounded and 3 missing. On the 22 we took
up position near Atlanta remaining there until the night of the
25th of Aug when we fell back with remainder of the Corps to
the Chattahoochia River to guard the bridges, Railroads &
supplies while the remainder of the Army started for the rear of
Atlanta.

The Company K Muster Roll repeats the above, with its own
version as follows.

July & Aug. 1864 Paces Ferry, Ga.
On the 2nd day of July this Company with the Reg't took
up its march in pursuit of the enemy who was then retreating
from the Kenesaw Mt. line. We skirmished with him at

---

[40]John Bell Hood, Confederate Corps Commander, who replaced Gen. Joseph
Johnston as Commander of the Confederate Troops defending Atlanta.
On July 17th, Jefferson Davis relieved Gen. Johnston, replacing him with Hood.

.

different times and took an active part in the battles of Peach Treek Creek on July 20th. On the 23rd we advanced and built works within one mile of Atlanta. Here we remained until August 25th when we moved to Paces Ferry on the Chattahoochie River where we remained until Muster day.

Again, returning to the 137th Regiment, N.Y.S.V. Muster Roll it continues with no entries other than dates and locations

Sept. 64 Atlanta, Ga.
Oct. 64 Atlanta, Ga
Nov. 64, Louisville, Ga.
Dec. 64, Savannah, Ga.

Continuing from the Regimental Field and Staff report, 1864 was brought to a close as follows

Sept. & Oct. 1864 Atlanta, Ga.
Oct. 31, 1864 The Reg't left Paces Ferry on the Chattahoochie River on the evening of Sept. 2nd 1864 and marching toward Atlanta entered that city about 12 oclock midnight with colors flying, drums beating, etc., etc. On the morning of the 3rd were stationed near the Macon Road in rear of a strong fort constructed by the Rebels and in case of attack were to support a Battery stationed there. On the morning of the 10th, David Ireland, Comd'g 3rd Brigade, 2nd Div., 20 Corps & Colonel of this (137th) Reg't died of Dysentary. From that time to the present the Regt has twice accompanied the Brigade on foraging expeditions into the interior 25 or 30 miles being absent each time not less than four days. Have moved camp not less than three times & latterly have been encamped with the entire Brigade on a line. Brigade dress parades have been held from time to time.

The Company K, Muster Roll is short.

September & October 1864 Atlanta, Ga.
On the 2nd day of Sept. 1864 we broke camp at Paces Ferry, Ga. and moved towards Atlanta. We entered the city about midnight where our Corps had some garrison duty until now.

That was the final descriptive entry in the Company K Muster Roll. The remaining bi-monthly sheets contained only the dates and locations of the reports.

November & December 1864   Savannah, Ga.
January & February, 1865   Near Nortons Tavern, S.C.
March & April, 1865   Raleigh, N.C.

The 137th Regimental Muster Roll Micro Film records concluded with the following dates and places.
Jan. 65 Sisters Ferry, Ga.
February 65, In the field, South Carolina
March 65, Near Goldsboro, NC
April 65, Raleigh, NC
May 65, Near Washington, DC

From the Field & Staff Report comes the only additional information found, on the activities of the 137th Regiment, N.Y.S.V. and this covers the remaining time until their muster out date, in mid 1865.

This report also parrallels recorded and published histories of Sherman's famous march to the sea. The 137th Regiment was one of the units involved in that march.

Nov. Dec. 1864   Savannah, Ga.
Dec. 31st, 1864 Remained at Atlanta until the 15th of Nov.

When we started on a campaign for the sea coast. We marched by way of Decatur, Social Circle, Madison arriving at Milledgeville Nov. 21. Thence passing through Sandersville, Davisboro, and to the left of Milles arriving in the rear of Savannah on the 10th of Dec. This Regt was deployed as skirmishers on the morning of the 11th and were the first to find the Rebel troops whose right rested on the Savannah River. Breastworks were thrown up on the afternoon of the same day and we lay there until the morning of the 21st Dec. When the evacuation of the city was discovered. This regt was the second Regt to enter the city. Distance marched on the campaign from Atlanta to Savannah about 320 miles.

During the entire duration of the march from Atlanta to Savannah, little was known, by the public in the North, as to where this army, commanded by General Sherman, was or what they were doing. Communications were slow in reaching the people at home and the Government in Washington. It was thought, by many, that these units would never reach their objectivie and an Army of this size could not make such a march through hostil country and survive.

General Sherman never meant for his Army to be supplied in the usual manner of supply trains and wagons. It was his intention to live off the land as they advanced. The Field and Staff report of January and February, 1865, contains some of the details regarding what the 137th New York Regiment did as their part.

Jan & Feb 1865

In the Field, S.C.   Feb 28, 1865

Remained in Savannah, Ga. Until Jan 27th when a new campaign was commenced. We marched to Sisters Ferry where we crossed the Savannah to South Carolina shore and commenced our march through that state destroying all public property and subsisting almost entirely off the country. Passed through Blacksville and on the 15th, Feb. this Regt skirmished into Lexington C. H., Youngsville and on the 28th of Feb., bivouacked near Finches Creek, S.C. Distance marched from Savannah to this point about 250 miles.

From the National Archives Library, and a "Compendium Of the War of The Rebellion" by Frederick H. Dyer, gives the following synopsis of the 137th Regiment, NYSV of their Civil War actions.

The regiment was organized at Binghampton, N.Y. and mustered into service September 25, 1862, left for Washington D.C on that same date and was attached to the 2nd Brigade, 1st Division, 12th Army Corps, Army of the Potomac to October 1862.and remained part of the 12th Army Corps until October 1863. At that time they were transferred to the 20th Army Corps as part of the Army of the Cumberland until June of 1865.

The 137th regiment saw service through out the Civil War arena, beginning in Harpers Ferry, Va., September 27-30, 1862. Duty at Bolivar Heights until December. Sent on reconnoissance to Rippon and Charlestown, W. Va., November 9. Reconnoissance to Winchester, Va., December 2-6. Charlestown and Berryville December 2. Marched to Fredericksburg, Va., Dec. 9-16. They were at Fairfax Station until April 27, 1863. They mad a "Mad March" to Charlottesville Campaign April 27-May 6. Battle of Chancellorsville May 1-5. Participated in Gettysburg (Pa) Campaign June 11- July 24including Battle of Gettysburg, July 1-3. Purssued Lee from Gettysburg to Manassas Gap, Va., July 5-24. Drew duty on line of the Rappahnnock until September. Movement to Bridgeport, Ala., September 24-October 4. Reopened Tennessee River October 26-29. Battle of Wauhatchie, Tenn., October 28-29. Chattanooga-Ringgold Campaign November 23-27. Lookout Mountain, November 23-24. Mission Ridge, November 25. Ringgold Gap, Taylor's Ridge, November 27. Duty at Bridgeport until May, 1864.

Atlanta (Ga.) Campaign, May 1 until September 8. Demonstration on Rocky Faced Ridge, May 8-11, Battle of Resaca. May 14-15. Neared Cassville May 19. Advanced on Dallas May 22-25. New Hope Church May 25. Battles around Dallas, New Hope Church and Allatoona Hills, May 26-June 5. Participated in operations around Marietta and against Kenesaw Mountain June 10-July 2 Among these were Pine Hill, June 11-14; Lost Mountain, June 15-17;

gilgal or Golgotha Church, June 15; Muddy Creek, June 17; Noyes' Creek, June 19; Kolb's Farm, June 22 (This is where Andrew H. Gale was killed). Assult on Kenesaw, June 27; Ruff's Station, Smyrna Camp Ground, July 4; Chattahoochie River, July 5-17; Peach Tree Creek, July 19-20. Siege of Atlanta, July 22-August 25. This was followed by Operations at Chattahoochie River Bridge August 26-September 2. Occupation of Atlanta September2-November 15. Expedition to Tuckum's Cross Roads, October 26-29.

Near Atlanta November 9. March to the sea, November 15-December 10. Near Davisboro, November 28. Siege of Savannah, December 10-21. Campaign of the Carolinas January to April, 1865. Averysboro, N.C., March 16. Battle of Bentonville March 19-21, occupation of Goldsboro, March 24. Advance on Raleigh, April 9-13 followed by the occupation of Raleigh, April 14, Bennett's House, April 26. Surrender of Joseph Johnson and his army.

March to Washington D.C via Richmond, Va., April 29-May 19. Grand Parade and Review May 24. The veterans and new recruits of the 137th Regiment NYSV were transferred to the 102nd New York Infantry June 1. The Regiment was mustered out June 9, 1865.

The 137th Regiment Infantry suffered the following casulties during their service.6 Officers and 121 Enlisted men killed and mortally wounded and 4 Officers and 163 Enlisted men by disease. Total lost, 294.

This Regiment covered the entire scope of the Civil War arena except for the far West, where there was not much fighting.

References

DeWitt Historical Society of Tompkins County, New York
Frederick H. Dyer, *A Compendium of the War of the Rebellion*
National Archives, Washington, D.C.
New York State Archives, Albany, New York
The Martin Memorial Library, York, Pennsylvania
The New York State Library, Albany, New York

INDEX

A

Acquia Landing, Va..25, 26

Ammanion, Dean 15

Antietum, Va. 75

Aquia Creek, Va 21, 23-25

Arlington House 61

Army of the Cumberland. 91, 99, 116

Army of the Potomac..25, 91, 98, 150

Ashby's Gap..76

Ashton, Oliver 75

Atlanta, Ga..153, 154, 163-169

Auburn, NY 10, 12, 57

B.

B & O Railroad.92, 93, 102.

Baltimore, Md..19, 21, 24, 61, 62, 77

Banks, Gen..4

Barton, NY 1

Bauldwin, Prof. 12

Bealton Station, Va..92, 93

Bea Line Creek..115

Bellaire, Ohio 91

Bentwood, Va. 93

Berryville, Va. 21

Binghampton, N.Y. 1

Blacksville, SC. 169

Bolliver Heights, Va. 2, 13, 21, 22

Bostwick, Ezra 8, 59, 63, 71, 72, 78, 81, 84. 85, 87, 88, 100,
        108, 111, 118, 121, 123, 129, 131, 133, 134,
        139, 146, 148, 151-153, 162, 164.

Bostwick, Harris 9, 10

Bostwick, Ruth 29

Bostwick, Stephen 10

Bragg, Gen. Braxton 115, 117, 128, 129, 131

Brandy Station 100

Briceville Md 25

Bridgeport, Ala..92, 93. 112, 143, 157

Brown, Biley 73

Bunker Hill, Va.,--22

C.

Calletts Station..76

Camp Douglas..6,

173

Candor, NY 1
Carlette Station, Va..80
Caroline, NY..1
Centerville, Ind..103
Chancellorsville, Va..23,25,
Charleston, SC..98
Charlestown, Va..21, 22
Charlestown, W Va..20
Chattahoochi River..165, 166
Chattanooga Creek..115, 128
Chattanooga, Tn..92, 93, 105, 115, 126, 127, 137, 139, 144,
        153, 157
Chenabgo, NY..1
Chickamanga River..126
Columbus, Oh..102
Company K. 137th Reg.NYSV..1,2,19, 27, 64, 70, 93, 117,
        143 , 148, 157, 165, 167
Conklin, NY..1
Corby, Col..21
Crainton Gap..76
Cranberry Summit..102
Culps Hill, Pa..62, 67
        D.
Dalton, Ga..152, 153, 157
Danby, NY. 1
Darne, Mary 39
Davisboro, Ga..168
Davison, John 73, 81, 122, 152
Davison, Mr. 10, 12
Decatur, Ga..168
Decker, Ala. 110
Delano, Gov. 15
Discord, Tn..92, 93
Driden News 80, 120, 137
Duck River 110
Dumfries, Va..20-25
        E.
Edwards Ferry, Va..24, 25
Eleventh Corp..76, 77, 79, 92, 93, 102, 109, 125, 137, 151
Elizabethtown, Ky..104
Elk River..110
Elmira, NY..60, 62
Ewell, Gen. Richard S..67
Ewell's Corps..68

Candor, NY 1

Carlette Station, Va..80

Caroline, NY..1

Centerville, Ind..103

Chancellorsville, Va..23,25,

Charleston, SC..98

Charlestown, Va..21, 22

Charlestown, W Va..20

Chattahoochi River..165, 166

Chattanooga Creek..115, 128

Chattanooga, Tn..92, 93, 105, 115, 126, 127, 137, 139, 144, 153, 157

Chenabgo, NY..1

Chickamanga River..126

Columbus, Oh..102

Company K. 137th Reg.NYSV..1,2,19, 27, 64, 70, 93, 117, 143 , 148, 157, 165, 167

Conklin, NY..1

Corby, Col..21

Crainton Gap..76

Cranberry Summit..102

Culps Hill, Pa..62, 67

D.

Dalton, Ga..152, 153, 157

Danby, NY. 1

Darne, Mary 39

Davisboro, Ga..168

Davison, John 73, 81, 122, 152

Davison, Mr. 10, 12

Decatur, Ga..168

Decker, Ala. 110

Delano, Gov. 15

Discord, Tn..92, 93

Driden News 80, 120, 137

Duck River 110

Dumfries, Va..20-25

E.

Edwards Ferry, Va..24, 25

Eleventh Corp..76, 77, 79, 92, 93, 102, 109, 125, 137, 151

Elizabethtown, Ky..104

Elk River..110

Elmira, NY..60, 62

Ewell, Gen. Richard S..67

Ewell's Corps..68

F.

Fairfax Court House, Va..22
Fairfax Station, Va..21-23, 25, 75
Fairmont, W Va..101
Fairplay, Md..76
Farmington, W. Va. 101
Federal Census 1860. 53
Fifteenth Corps. 154
Finches Creek, SC..169
Forest Church, Ga..152
Fort Sumpter, SC..9
Fosterville, Tn..92, 93, 111
Fourth Division..152
Franklin, Ind..104
Frederick City, Md..4, 24, 75, 76
Fredericksburg,Va..24, 99
Freemont, W Va..101

G.

Galatin, Ky..105
Gale, Agusta 2, 14, 29, 31, 86, 152, 162-164
Gale, Andrew H..2, 3, 6, 9, 10, 12-14, 16-19, 23, 27, 29, 30,
          34, 51, 52, 63, 64, 70, 74-76, 78, 80, 85, 86,
88, 89, 93, 101, 104-106, 120, 125, 132, 134,
139-141, 144, 145, 147-150, 152-158, 160-
162, 164
Gale, Chloe..2, 9, 10, 17, 28, 85, 87-89, 98, 145
Gale, Peter B..2, 3, 6, 8, 9, 11, 12, 16, 17, 29, 53, 85-87, 98,
          163, 164
Gale, Scott 2, 9, 29
Geary, Gen. John White..20, 87, 129, 134, 135, 140
Georgetown, Va..80
Gettysburg, Pa..19, 62, 65-67, 70, 71, 76
Goldsboro, NC..167
Goose Creek, Va..63, 77
Grafton, W Va..101
Grant, Gen. Ulysses S..127, 128, 150
Greenleaf, Samuel 10
Greenlick, Bill 35
Green Spa, Va..21
Greenwich, Va..76
Groton, NY..1, 2, 10, 11, 14, 19, 23, 27, 29, 34, 41, 42, 51,
          61-64, 70, 94, 95, 139, 143, 144, 146, 151,
          154, 156, 160, 162

H.

Harper's Ferry, Va. 2, 16, 19, 23, 29, 76, 101, 102
Harrisburg, Pa..61, 62
Heath, Andrew 15, 73
Hillsboro, Va. 21, 22, 80
Hood, Gen. John B..165
Hooker, Gen. Joseph. 115, 116, 128, 137, 151, 153
Hunter, Gen..129

I.

Igafs, Reuben 10
Indianapolis, Ind. 92, 93, 104
Ireland, Col. David..1, 5, 166
Ithica, NY..1, 39, 62

J.

Jackson, Gen. Thomas J. (Stonewall). 4
Jeffersonville, In. 93, 104
Jeffersonville, Md. 75, 76
Jones Cross Road 75

K.

Kelly, Fitch 38
Kelly's Ford, Va. 24, 76, 91, 93, 99
Kemper's Ford, Va. 68, 70, 76, 80-82, 84, 86, 89, 91, 94, 97
Kenesaw Mt., Ga. 157, 165
King, Helen 10, 30, 31
King, Norman 15
Kirkwood, NY..1
Knopp, Iseral 37
Knoxville, Md. 7, 24
Krenselman, Gen..62

L.

Lazelle, David 32
Leesburg, Va. 22, 24
Lexington Court House, NC..169
Lincoln, President Abraham..1
Lisle, NY..1
Littlestown, Pa. 24, 65, 68, 76
Lookout Creek, Tn. 115, 117, 135
Lookout Mt., Tn. 92, 93, 117, 119, 125, 126, 128, 132, 133
Lookout Valley, Tn..91, 115, 13
Lost Mt., Ga..158
Louisville, Ga. 104, 166
Louisville, Ky. 92, 93
Ludlow, George 34
Ludlow, Harriet 35

Ludlw, John 5, 15, 73
        M.
Madison, Ga..168
Maine, NY..1
Major, Wilobey 37
Manassas Gap, Va. 76, 80
Marietta, Ga..154, 156, 157, 159, 160, 162, 163, 165
Martinsburg, Va..101
McGrawville, NY 38
Meade, Maj. Gen. George G..69
Middleburg, Md. 76
Milan, NY. 31, 55, 146
Milledgeville, Ga..168
Milles, Ga.168
Missionary Ridge, Tn. 115, 126, 128
Mission Ridge. 117
Monocacy River. 24
Murfreesboro, Tn. 92, 93, 108, 109
        N.
Nashville, Tn..92, 93, 105-109, 139, 147, 150
National Archives..1
New Hope Church, Ga..156
New Orleans, La. 5
New York, NY. 74
New York State Archives..1
None Such, Tn..123
Norton's Tavern, SC..167
        O.
Ocauquion River. 21
Occoquan River 22, 23
Ohio Central R.R. 92, 93
Ohio River. 92, 93, 102, 104
100th Regt. NYSV. 10
102nd. Regt. NYSV 140
111th Regt. NYSV..6, 15
111th Regt. PV..95
160th Regt. NYSV..15
137th Regt. NYSV. 1, 2, 8, 19, 21, 23, 27, 29, 59, 62, 64, 65,
        70, 74, 76, 99, 106, 113, 115, 128, 143, 156-
158, 162, 164, 166, 167, 169
Oswego, NY..1, 60, 62
        P.
Pace's Ferry, Ga..165-167
Peach Tree Creek..165, 166

Pea Vine Creek, Tn..117
Perkins, Libby 56
Petersville..24
Pick, Aaron 3
Piedmont, Va..80
Pleasant Valley, Md..73, 76
Point of Rocks..24, 76
Potomac River..24
         R.
Raccoon Ford, Va..92, 93
Raccoon Mt., Tn..115, 117, 130
Raleigh, NC..167
Rapidan River..24, 25, 92
Rappahannick River..24, 25, 76, 80, 94
Resacoa, Ga..157
Rhoresville, Md..75
Richford, NY..1
Richmond, In..103, 104
Richmond, Va..144
Ringold, Ga. 115, 117, 126, 152
Rippon, Va. 19
Roberts, Chaplin E.F..158, 160
         S.
Sandersville, Ga..168
Sandy Hook, Va. 4
Sanford, NY..1
Sarakonn, Mary 39
Savannah, Ga..166-169
Savannah River..168, 169
2nd Brigade. 65
Second Division..91, 166
Seventy Third Regt. 77
Sharpsburg, Md..76
Sharpstein, John 8, 43
Shelbyville, Tn..9, 92, 108, 109
Shelmound, Al..93
Shell Mound. 92, 97
Sherman, Maj. Gen. William T. 128, 129, 157, 162, 164, 169
Shipman, Capt..99
Sister Ferry, Ga..167, 169
Sixtieth Regt, NY. 155
Sixty Sixth Ohio Regt. 135
Slocum, Gen. 105
Smith, Frank 30, 41

Smith, Gen. 105
Snickers Gap. 76, 80
Social Circle, Ga..168
Spencer, NY..1
Stafford Court House, Va..23-25
Stevenson, Al. 92, 112, 139, 143, 144, 146, 148, 150, 151,
        154, 156, 157, 163
Stoneman's Switch..34
Strasburg, Va..21
Stuart's Cavalry. 21-23
Sundy Hook..4
        T.
Taneytown, Md..76
Taylor Ridge..115
Tennessee River 112
Third Brigade. 91, 166
Third Division 152
Third Regiment..157
Thoroughfare Gap..76
Triangle, NY..1
Tullahoma, Tn. 92, 93, 110
Twelfth Corps. 91, 102, 109, 137, 152
Twentieth Corps. 91, 113, 116, 128, 143, 151, 152, 157, 162,
        164, 166
Twenty-Ninth Regt. NYSV 134
        U.
Union, NY. 1
United States Ford..24
        V.
Van Vorhees, Lt. Col..92
        W.
Walkerville..24
Wallace, James..29
Warrington Junction, Va..77-79
Wartract, Tn..111
Washington, DC. 15, 61-63, 73-76, 78, 79, 92, 93, 98, 101,
        106, 164, 167, 169
Waterford, Va..76
Wauhatchee Junction, 93..-
Wauhatchee River..125
Wauhatchee. Tn..112, 115, 117, 143
Westbourough 25
West Point, NY 117
Wheeling, W. Va. 92

White Plains, Va..76, 77
Whitesides, Ala. 135, 143
Williamsport, Pa. 61
Wilson, Daniel 39
Winchester, Va..20-22
Windson, NY. 1
          Y.
Youngsville, SC 169

ABOUT THE AUTHOR

Richard T. Gillespie was born May 28, 1930, in York, Pennsylvania. His family lived in the Borough of West York and he graduated from West York High School in 1948. Having grown up only twenty-five miles east of Gettysburg, Pennsylvania, the American Civil War became his favorite subject.

He attended Pennsylvania State University, majoring in Business and History, and entered the business world in television broadcasting in 1952. He worked in three television stations over an eight-year span, before putting his education to use in the industrial sales field.

In the 1970s he started a business that specialized in antique and estate jewelry, and that field took him to many antique auctions. These auctions inspired him to pursue Civil War artifacts and led him to compile this book.

In 1992 he retired, turning his jewelry store over to his daughter and her husband. Retirement allowed him the time required to do the research and write this book.

In addition to this book, he has started two others and hopes to have them published in another year.

Even though he turned seventy-five years old in May of 2005, he plans to keep going and possibly develop more books on historical subjects.